Being Locked-Up: Prisoner's Stories

Cashville

By:

Russell McKinnon

To: Marnie
Date: 7-5-2025
From: Russell McKinnon

Russell McKinnon

Copyright © R. McKinnon
March 2020

All right reserved. No part of this book may be reproduced in any form, or by any means without prior consent of the author and publisher as a collective, except brief quotes used in reviews.

Book Production: Crystell Publications
You're The Publisher, We're Your Legs
We Help You Self Publish Your Book

BOP E-mail ONLY – cleva@crystalstell.com
E-Mail – minkassitant@yahoo.com
Website: www.crystellpublications.com
(405) 414-3991

Printed in the USA

FOREWARD

The number of inmates returning to jail, state, and federal prison within three years of release has remained steady for more than a decade. This is a strong indication that the prison systems are failing to deter criminals from reoffending, a new study has concluded.

In one of the more comprehensive reports of its kind, The Pew Research Center on state level found that slightly more than four in 10 offenders return to prison within three years, a collective rate that has changed in recent years despite high increase in prison spending, which is now costing states over $82-billion annually.

The system designed to deter (inmates) from continued criminal behavior clearly is falling short, according to the study by Pew's Public Safety Performance Project, an arm of the non-profits public policy analysis group.

"That is an unhappy reality, not just for offenders but for the safety of American communities".

The group analyzed full of partial data provided by 41 states for inmates released in 2004 and for prisoner leaving in 2008, over two decades now. By 2012 slightly more than 55% of the second group return. Of the 33 states that provided data for both periods 15 reported recidivism rates had increased by much as 30% by 2015.

Among them:

>In South Dakota, the return rate rose 35% in 2007.

>In Washington State reported a 31% jump during the same period.

>In Minnesota's rate increased 11% and by 2007 the state posted the highest prisoner return rate of all participating states at 61.2%. This is double in percentage the amount of people returning

back to jail and prison all across America.

We are in the beginning of 2019 and the prison on all levels local, state, federal and juvenile, is busting out the seam with overcrowding conditions.

Since the mid-80's annual state and federal costs have risen from $10 billion to 52 billion, according to Pew Research Center, which was reported in 2007.

Right now, when offenders on (Probation or Parole) are breaking the rules, supervision agencies win by sending them back to prison and getting them off their caseloads. That needs to be flipped, so agencies get rewarded with a share of the savings when they reduce returns to prison.

Experts say, "there's not enough money being placed in the prevention and drug rehabilitation centers for low-level drug users, and there are few-to-no jobs for felons who sell drugs to be replaced". Who's going to fix this problem that faces America?

Obviously, the Republicans would not allow Obama to do much. The petty crimes and the Crack ratio 18-to-1 is still injustice and overflowing the Prison system.

By the stroke of his mighty executive pen President Obama could have reduced the unfair and disproportionate sentences that African American's and other minorities receive in these American biased courtrooms before leaving office. For those of us who are fighting for the freedom and justice don't be afraid of going to jail, because if they know you're afraid of jail, then that's where they like to send you.

Acknowledge/Dedication:

First and foremost, I give Thanks and Honor to "God, The Most-High" for giving me another chance at Life. When I had no one in my corner to comfort me, I could always turn to Him.

I want to give Thanks to all my family who stood by me during my Incarceration. Both deceased, My Beautiful and wonderful Mother Beatrice Mckinnon, and my Awesome wise Father, Archie Ewing McKinnon: To all my Beautiful Sisters: Petrina McKinnon, Tammie McKinnon, Juanita Rucker, Obbie Holt, Marsh "Big Red" McKinnon R.I.P. Daina McKinnon. "Shout out to My brother's "R.I.P." Claude Rucker, "R.I.P." Frederick "Nitemare" Adam, and Carl "Phil-fashion" McKinnon, My Nephew's "Andre Rucker, Derrick Rucker, Phillip Hamer, Mantez McKinnon and Jonathan Corley a Future Music/Film Producer star on the rise. My Nieces, "R.I.P. Tiara "Fly" Booker". Shout out to Quanisha Morgan, Keosha McKinnon, Donaisa Hockett, and Kemiya Mckinnon, got to give her a special shout out, for helping me operate this laptop computer :)

"A Very...Very Warm Special Thanks: to the Wonderful Woman in my life that's been holding me down, through thick and thin". My Beautiful Black Queen Ms. Starla Nunn. Thank you, 'Baby' for putting up with all my aggravation at times when I got on your nerves...You my heart and soul...The Sun don't shine without you!

Big Shout out to all My "R.G.'s Comrades, Y'all know who y'all are. What's understood doesn't have to be explained.

Shout out to "Lil Dro Deuce, aka...Tha' Badguy", you kept it "To Real"...and gave me a helping hand when no one else did... Raymond Clay, Lil Les, L.T., Stephon Rose, "Freeway The Real Ricky Ross, and A Special Thanks to my great friend and/mentor from Philly who inspired me to write literature, one helluva book author: James "Jimmy Da Saint" Mathis, you truly inspired me bro;

"Special Thanks to the publisher's, and editors. Everyone that had a task in bringing this work of art into fruition. Thank you all sincerely, for your time and efforts...

"If I didn't mention you on this acknowledgement page, don't charge it to my heart, charge it to my mind, it's just too many people to remember everyone. God Bless, Peace Out!"

INTRODUCTION

There are over 2,000,000 Men, Women, and Children locked up in this so-called "great" country that we know as America. Question: Why is it that the most powerful country in the world has more prisons than any other country on the face of this earth?

There are more prisons in America than Great Britain, Canada, and Japan combined. Truth be told, there will never be fair justice, equality, freedom, and peace in this country until its constitutional principles are fully applied to ALL citizens. The only way that a new America can be born is to completely dismantle the racism and hatred held against Black, Native, and Hispanic people in these unfair courtrooms here in America and all the measures used to enforce it.

Being locked up not only robs you of your freedom, but it attempts to take away your very being and unique identity. Everyone in prison wears the same uniform, eats the same food, drinks the same water, and follows the same schedule and rules. It is by definition a purely authoritarian state that tolerates no independence, privacy, or individuality. As conscious individuals, men and women are aware of right and wrong. We as convicted felons must fight against the prison's attempts to rob any one of these qualities from us. I know that no sacrifice is too great in the quest and struggle for freedom.

No matter how high a Black man advances in this country, he will always be considered inferior to the lower white man. It isn't the lack of ability that limits Black, Native, and Hispanic people, but rather the lack of opportunity.

In this Book there are some real interesting stories of prisoner's sharing their experiences. "Being Lockup: Prisoner Stories", tells events that affect many lives.

My Name is Cashville, I am the author of this book "Being Lockup: Prisoner Stories". My time spent while incarcerated has broadened my horizons. I've seen life at its most pitiless, and I am now a true revolutionary fighter for freedom and justice. I pledge to free the minds of the incarcerated, and to liberate all people from the continuing suffering and bondage of poverty, deprivation, injustice, and other forms of discrimination. Our wellbeing as a collective—not as individuals—is what matters the most.

To be free in a society is not merely to cast off those physical chains, handcuffs, and shackles, but instead to live in a way that respects and enhances the freedom of others. The graph of improvement in prisons is never steady. Progress will always be halting, and typically accompanied by setbacks and roadblocks. People sitting on Death Row for decades waiting on their execution date, appeal, or an advancement might take years to win. And even after they've secured that victory that motion could be rescinded in one day.

Time waits for no one. Time may seem to stand or set still for most of us in prison, but it does not stop for those on the outside. Prison can rob you of your freedom and steal away your youth, but it can never take away your memories. As you read further through this book you will get a glimpse inside the minds of men who are surrounded by madness and destitution. They want us to stay stagnant as we sit and waste between steel and stone. This is why it's important that we surround ourselves with the type of individuals who keep the fire burning in our minds and hearts, while we are incarcerated under the tremendous weight of isolation. We have to believe and know that there's more to life than this miserable existence.

We live this artificial life with our backs against the wall, in a place where we've come to know loneliness, learning the lessons of pain, while becoming comrades of the struggle. Some of us will never make it out of this human warehouse alive, and some will end up losing their minds in here. But nevertheless, we still strive for truth and real knowledge. We strive for real human connection and a meaningful life. And we strive for these things with true radical passion, and with the understanding that we are against all odds.

For some, life is cheap, meaningless, and pretty much determined. People like that can't be helped until they choose to alleviate themselves from the path of self-destruction. But for those who keep resistance in their hearts, they will never stop striving and will never give up, because there is something inside of them that lets them know that life, freedom, and truth is something worth fighting for. Each day that we wake-up and open our eyes to a new day is an act of resistance.

It doesn't matter whether you were born rich or poor, black, white, red, brown, or yellow. You and I may be different in race, culture, nationality, and socioeconomic status, but we all have one thing in common in Prison, and that is we are all living, breathing human beings. No matter what you are in prison for, we all have the gift of life. Each of us was conceived by destiny, produced by purpose, and packaged with potential to live a meaningful and fulfilling life. Deep within each of us lies natural talents and gifts to manifest our God-given potential.

We must be conscious of where our lives are headed. Sometimes I have to ask myself these questions: Have I assessed my life lately? Have I looked at where I'm going? Have I asked myself, where I want to go? These are true inner-self questions a conscious minded person cannot ignore. "It is never too late to take charge of my life" is what I tell myself every day. I consistently search for that seed of greatness within me and make sure that I share it someone whenever I can.

Question; Can prisoner's change? Self-Improvement is all about change and growth. We're identifying things that we would like to be different in our lives, and then taking action to effect those changes. But, if you're like me, you've tried changing some things in the past and found yourself slipping back into old habits. That challenge is enough to make you wonder if lasting change is truly possible. I'm here to assure you that it is!

Change is a lengthy process that doesn't happen overnight. It requires hard work, conscientiousness, willpower, sacrifice, dedication, and great discipline. How often have you said to yourself, "I'm going to think only positive thoughts from now on", or "I've got to quit smoking these cigarettes", "I've got to lose this weight". Then just a few minutes later, you realize you've broken your resolution. When this happens, it's easy to get discouraged and feel that change is impossible. It is not enough to just *want* to change or even to decide to change. Too often we expect that this will be enough, but these are just the first steps in that process.

Old habits do not readily let go just because we've

decided to change. Real change takes consistent effort, time, and determination. It often involves some discomfort as we move out of our comfort zone. Change produces withdrawal pains. Those of us who are willing and able to produce real change have learned to expect this and to prepare to take on the struggle that comes along with our transformation. In order to keep from slipping back into our comfort zone, we must keep the pressure up every day for an ample amount of time.

Example: If you are trying to change negative thought patterns and become a more upbeat, optimistic person, it may seem daunting to say, "for the next 14-days, I will never have a negative thought." But we can do it for an hour, or one day at a time. A little at a time, inch-by-inch, day-by-day, anything is possible. If we can keep up this consistent, daily effort for at least 14-days, we have a great chance of making the new habit stick. Once this happens, we have created lasting change…

CHAPTER 1

Crime, Criminal and Incarceration

Crime

Crime. What exactly is crime? This is a word that is mentioned often in our society, but what does it really mean? First, I am going to give you the dictionary term of the word *crime* and then I am going to give it to you from a criminal's perspective or my own point-of-view. The dictionary defines the word *crime* as: "a serious violation of law". My definition of the word *crime* is: "an activity that pays in many ways". Done well or on a large scale, crime can pay major dividends. Done perfectly, and a criminal could end up living a lavish lifestyle of the rich and famous, a life most dream of.

The only problem is a crime never registers as perfect until, the life of the criminal is over or until the day he dies. The only thing a criminal can do is hope and imagine that he has gotten away with the crime once he or she has committed one. Time eases their apprehension and years erase valuable evidence, but the mind and conscience always haunt the average criminal. Sometimes though, crime pays an immediate and exact revenge on the committed. This is the offender who goes out in a blaze of glory or is locked up under the jailhouse. This is the criminal who finds out that he is like a small fish swimming in a pool with hungry sharks.

The spoils are never enjoyed. They always eventually bring about a worse state of being that existed in the life of the criminal before he even decided to take part in the act in the first place. This is the crime that is never worth committing...

Criminal

Criminal, as defined by the dictionary is: "one who commits a crime". Criminals come in all shapes, forms, and fashion. It is not easy to identify a criminal. You have criminals from every element of life: petty small-time criminals, white collar criminals, and then big kingpins, drug lords, or cartel leaders that do billions of dollars' worth of crime. The biggest question of all questions that I would like everyone to ask themselves is "who are the real criminals?" For me, the answer to this question is very simple.

The real criminals are the people in this country who are in very high places and positions at the top of government policy and secret society. Most of the biggest criminals convene in various locations around the world. America itself has been involved in some of the biggest criminal enterprises in the world. One in particular was the Atlantic Slave Trade. America will never admit that slavery was ever a crime against humanity. Our African blood soaks the Native-land grounds of America that the Europeans stole from the Native people/Indians.

"If Slavery is a crime, then we must call America who she really is a criminal...To kidnap a people and to bring them into a strange land to be made a slave. Murdering, stealing, and selling human-beings like a piece of live-stock, merchandise or property, that's a crime in itself and the penalty for those crimes should be death". Who are the real criminals?

Incarceration

Incarceration is defined in the dictionary as "imprisonment". Incarceration as we know it to be today is simply modern-day slavery. Prison is nothing but a human-warehouse. It's a billion—if not trillion—dollar industry, which is why America has so many prisons.

I will admit that incarceration in the physical sense is sometimes necessary only to separate those who prey on society at large or refuse to obey the laws set forth by a governing authority. When a guilty man faces incarceration, he must decide whether he is as lowly as the deed he committed, or if in fact, he is better than his mistake.

A man who realizes that his worth is greater than the tag of "Criminal" that society places upon him, will find within him the dignity and desire to become free from mental incarceration. As a matter of fact, a wealth of thought will make him even more dangerous to those who have designed the system that thrives on a pattern of over-incarceration. The man who can accomplish that feat is gifted and will never be imprisoned again mentally or physically.

CHAPTER 2

Determination and Faith

Determination

Determination. Why is this word so important for incarcerated men and women, and exactly what does it mean? The dictionary defines *determination* as, "the act of deciding or fixing, having a firm purpose". To me, determination describes what it takes to survive in a cold and unforgiving world. Determination, plus a gift of courage, is what allows you to flourish.

The world inside of a prison setting is full of individuals who are determined to survive or merely exist. The prison industrial complex flourishes by making a fortune off of backs of prisoners, who are paid slave labor wages for their work.

The prison officials make the rules and hold the golden key to our freedom. However, many men and women throughout the prison system still keep that spark of determination lit inside of their hearts and minds. They are determined to someday get out of prison to go home and be with their loved ones.

At the end of each day, the quest and fight for freedom takes a great will of determination. Motivation will get you started, but it is determination that will keep you going.

<u>Faith</u>

Faith. What is *faith*? What does *faith* mean? According to the Webster Dictionary, *faith* means: "belief and trust in God, or a thing; a system of religious beliefs; supreme confidence".

Faith can take you a long way. In the worst of times, especially in prison, faith can be all a person has to hold on to while dealing with so much wickedness. The creator appreciates someone who still holds on to their faith, in spite of the many tests thrown at them.

Experiences—good and bad—are often the results of works of men themselves, happenstance, or of transgressions against him by another. The way a man handles himself through those experiences shows what kind of heart and faith he has.

True faith walks hand and hand with heart. Tell me someone who can survive without either in this sunless cemetery that warehouses human beings like livestock cattle.

CHAPTER 3

Misery and Destiny

Misery

Misery. Misery means "suffering and want caused by distress or poverty". We've all heard the old saying "That old coon there is a miserable guy". And if there's one thing about misery that we all know is that it loves company.

Misery is a terrible condition to be in. I've seen so many men in prison miserable and drowning in a sea of misery. Some have reasons different than others; the amount of time they have to serve, the stress of not being able to help their family or having an insufficient amount of funds on your books to afford basic amenities. Misery is so detrimental that it can destroy the heart and soul of a prisoner.

There is no such thing as joy, hope, or peace wherever misery dwells. Misery is contagious in nature, so if you don't make sure your resistance is strong you will catch it like an airborne disease.

Destiny

Destiny. Destiny means "that which is to happen in the future". Destiny rules us all. There is no sense being afraid of what lies and waits around the corner. Whether it is good or evil, it will be there waiting patiently no matter what. There is no sense trying to run, hide, duck, or go in a different direction. If you have prepared yourself spiritually and physically, you have already done all you can. Neither prayers nor weapons of man will guarantee survival.

God, for his own reasons that are unknown to man, will sometimes allow the wretched and evil to thrive and dominate, and yet let the good die young or allow them to suffer incessantly.

CHAPTER 4

Influence and Lust

Influence

Influence means "power or capacity of causing an effect in direct or in tangible ways". Here in Prison, influence is vital for survival. Shot-callers, spokespersons, or gang leaders all have the necessary influence to make decisions that affect your very existence. Influence is often displayed for negative purposes as opposed to positive purposes in this environment. Negative influence can get another man's life taken simply at the request of a respected shot-caller. A lot of crash dummies in here will try to make a name for themselves by being manipulated by influence.

Influence is really power by a less imposing name. When it is used for good purposes, influence can help to change and rebuild lives that would otherwise be lost. On the other hand, negative influence can sidetrack or demolish the lives of all those susceptible to its reaches. Leaders who wrongfully misguide or misdirect those who follow them will cause suffering and eventually devastation to their followers.

I advise any man, especially a young person, to be careful who they listen to and follow. Bad influence can cause you a great set-back or death behind these gloom filled prison walls.

Lust

Lust by dictionary terms means, "intense sexual desire; intense longing". Lust for money, power, or sex all lead to the same road—out in the middle of hell. Once the desire for any of those things becomes the focal point of a man's existence, he then plots his destination for that very end. When he begins to find excitement on his journey, he is quickening his pace.

Some are fortunate enough to crash on the way and have the sense to turn back. Smart money says that right now, sitting in purgatory, are probably those who enjoyed such a smooth ride to self-destruction that the only thing that they will agree on is that they never once thought about turning back.

Be careful what you lust for. Money and women's bodies are the most sought-after vices and the one sin. We all need money to survive, but it's the lust for money that is the root of all evil.

In Prison, lust can lead to all types of disasters. Lusting off a female staff/correctional officer can cause a man to unconsciously pull out his penis and masturbate on that woman. An act like that can get you sent to the "hole", or worse can cause a violent confrontation between you and another prisoner.

CHAPTER 5

Construction and Religion

Construction

Construction means "to build or make". Ironically, construction starts with its antithesis: destruction. Nothing can be built without something having been torn apart first. Even with thoughts and dreams, everything that discourages and causes self-doubt must be eliminated before the building process can begin. It's just like how the forest has to be destroyed so the city can be built.

In prison, a man should always focus on construction to build himself up while passing time. Free your mind to be creative. Victory is never built up until the wall of fear crumbles. It is most important to remain constant in construction or one becomes the victim of destruction.

Religion

Religion. Religion means, "service and worship of God; set or system of religious beliefs". Religion has been around since the beginning of time. To me, it has almost nothing to do with faith. Contrast to what most experts on theology understand, there is a religion that is widely accepted across the globe that transcends ethnicity, race, or gender. That religion has more followers than Christianity, Islam, Buddhism, and Judaism combined.

That religion is self-indulgence. It is widely accepted because human-beings are programmed to try this religion of comfort first. Nearly every human tries a religion based on faith at some point because they feel the sickening void that self-indulgence never satisfies. However, in the end, they almost always come back to practicing self-indulgence.

In the end, whatever people choose to love most eventually becomes their religion: money, power, sex, fame, cars, or drugs. Whatever religion you choose, please don't let it lead you to a grave.

CHAPTER 6

Sanity and Fear

Sanity

Sanity means, "soundness of mind". If you ask me, sanity is overrated. Nearly every great mind and figure in history has prospered directly from their own *insanity* or thrived in spite of their own sanity. The first man to volunteer himself to walk across the moon was probably insane because of the fact no man before him has done it before.

No matter what, to reach your goals requires a little insanity on your part. Just ask the college kid who came up with an innovative idea that made him richer than every oil baron, sultan, king, or real estate tycoon to ever live. Or how about the fatherless child from the projects and ghettoes of America who uses his wits, guts, and grit to become successful.

Jay-Z did it, and a few more music moguls succeeded against all odds. We have a brilliant brain power... it's time to use it. I've seen men go insane in these prisons and eat their own feces because they couldn't cope. I've seen men strive here due to their sanity. I have a motto: "I'll go anywhere on the face of this earth, except for going crazy or insane".

Fear

Fear. We all know what this word means. Fear is the most primal instinct known to man. Baby animals without any experience of death, cling to their parents because they know for some reason that it is the smartest and natural thing to do. The adult animal naturally knowns what can happen and guards its young out of fear of extinction.

The law of nature programs animals to respond to fear naturally by flight. A seal will never attack a shark just as a gazelle will never attack a lion. Animals only fight when confronting a natural enemy that their instincts tell them they can defeat or if flight is impossible. Humans are the only creatures who attempt to face their fears for the sake of what they may gain from victory.

Most find out that they had that fear for a good reason, but by then it's often too late. There's a lot of fear in being in prison, especially behind the walls of high security level penitentiaries where the violence level is very high. Men in prison will kill out of fear. My pops used to tell me this a long time ago, "son, they don't bury the scared, they bury the dead.

CHAPTER 7

Dreams and Anger

Dreams

Dreams. Dreams are defined as a, "series of thoughts or visions during sleep". Dreams are the most mysterious part of the human psyche. People work hard to put themselves in the best position imaginable, but even when they achieve what is perceived to be the ultimate that life has to offer, most still dream of much more. There is a line where a euphoric reality actually crosses over into fantasy, and just across that line is where the senses are overloaded with thoughts of pleasure, feelings, and sensations that can't be captured by reality.

There is also a dark space where dreams gone wrong lie in wait. They are born from the pangs of anxiety, fear, guilt, self-hate and evil. Those dreams rip through the being of children and men alike. They become a nightmare so bad that even waking up doesn't stop the effects.

Prisoners dream about someday walking out the front door to freedom. No impudence intended; this isn't a joking matter. The shoe could easily be on the other foot. You and I, we all dream in one way or another. Some prisoners sit around and daydream all day long as a pastime activity.

Anger

Anger. We all know how this word feels. Emotions such as frustration, jealousy, pride, disgust, sadness, anxiety, and other unpleasant emotions often disguise themselves through anger. Anger easily lends itself to projection. The formula is as easy as one, two, three... *get angry, blame someone, and attack.* Somehow, someway, the anger must be let loose, even if it's on yourself. There are anger management programs and classes here in prison that a lot of prisoner's are required to take to deal with their anger problems.

Don't let your anger consume you. There are many men behind these walls that are only here because of their inability to control their anger.

CHAPTER 8

Greed and Fantasies

Greed

Greed means "selfish desire beyond reason". Greed and unlawful acquisition are never far apart. Once the spirit of greed has taken over a man, he begins to plot on treasures that he has no rightful claims to. Greed pushes a man to break the laws of the state, nature, or God to obtain whatever he desires such as money, power, women, or fame. Often, when you're consumed by greed you can't see that what you're doing is wrong. It's like a horse set off on a path with blinders on unknowingly headed for a cliff with the devil as his passenger.

The only way he can survive is if he somehow turns back. However, if the greed is too overwhelming then that man is headed for certain disaster.

Here in Prison, you see a lot of greed in the men we interact with on a day to day basis. Greed over small, petty things like a postal stamp can drive a prisoner to commit murder.

Fantasies

Fantasies. What is a fantasy? The dictionary defines fantasy as "imagination, or product of the imagination".

Fantasies are as close to reality than most people ever dare to dream. There is an imaginary line created by society that separate most people from their dreams. The world teaches people to be average, but only applauds those who excel its simple logic. Without the normal, the extraordinary can't shine. Choosing to make your fantasies reality is much more difficult than living a life of normalcy.

It's up to each individual to decide what their fantasies are. Not everyone desires a life of fame and fortune. However, everyone should strive and drive themselves forward towards living his or her ultimate purpose. Also, keep in mind that the best part of the fantasy isn't the destination…it's the journey.

For a lot of prisoners incarcerated most of these men and women have their minds set to try to live out their fantasies. I hear men sit around every day, all day sharing fantasized lies with one another, "Yeah man, when I was out there in the free world, I had a Lamborghinis, Ferraris, yachts, jets, etc." These men are lying through their teeth. They can't even make commissary. They just love to lie and fantasize about wealth and fame.

CHAPTER 9

Love and Intuition

Love

What is love? Love is "strong affection; warm attachment; or enjoying something greatly". Love is by far the most powerful emotion. Most people long for it, yet, never invite it into their lives. Some love junkies get a small taste of it and crave more than they can afford. No matter what people say, like everything else in life love has a cost.

Love is an emotion that demands all of your attention and spotlight. It is the most mysterious emotion of all, and the most difficult to control. Not answering love's call will cause it to wither and die, or worse shatter into pieces of jealousy, rage, hurt, anger, and sometimes vengeance. However, if nurtured properly love can make a man feel like dancing.

Real good love is like a favorite song of yours that never stops playing. In Prison, love is the rarest emotion displayed by cold-hearted, closed-minded individuals who are usually angry, frustrated, bitter, and miserable due to being confined to a cage-like prison cell. Prison is efficient in stealing away the joy, dignity, integrity, and happiness of all those that are trapped behind its walls.

But love is the medicine to a broken heart or a sick man's illness.

Without love the spirit is fragile and broken.

Intuition

What is intuition? Intuition means, "quick and ready insight". Intuition is the vision mastered with the third eye. Unfortunately, most people are too preoccupied with seeing things through their two physical eyes only. This doesn't allow them to see beyond the surface of things. The third eye takes in messages from that which is unseen, including energy, good fortune, and especially danger.

A highly developed sense of intuition is the reason why certain people appear to be lucky or undeservingly prosperous. The simple phrase, "I can feel it", is not a mere saying. It is the mantra of those who are watching with the third eye. "Don't go out tonight", "Turn left instead of right", You hear the voice and heed not the message. The next moment or day you say "Damn, if I had not gone out that night that could have been me". There's no sure thing as coincidence. It's just happenstance created by those who see with the third eye and those who choose to listen to or ignore its message.

Only the strong survive in a jungle amongst gorillas, apes, lions, and any other predatory killer you can think of. Here in prison, the instincts in the back of your mind will alert you to danger whenever it's lurking. A wise man's conscience will let him know when something out of the ordinary is happening in and around him. That intuition will quickly kick in and save your life.

CHAPTER 10

Order

What does order mean? Order means, "rank, class, or special group; arrangement; rule of law; authoritative regulation or instruction."

Order is the way in which the master of all creation operates. For everything that must happen, happens divinely. What good is it to question why something happens? There is no answer for such a question.

To be a true servant of the creator is to not only accept the lesson of life, but to embrace them with one's whole heart. It would be foolish to consider life's harshest teachings enjoyable by any stretch. They are often painful and disheartening at the very least. The joy comes in the knowledge that order will bring positive from negative because it has to. Having the knowledge of the fact that through living in acceptance of God's order, means understanding that the unbearable has meaning and that all pain has purpose. Personal growth will allow it to be understood that wrong doings must exist so that good can reveal itself as the order of the creator.

In prison there has to be order set in motion to keep the peace between two prison cars, the administration, and individuals. Without order being administered, conflict and chaos will occur, and the outcome of a situation can result in a bloody confrontation. It happens all the time on these prison yards, state and local jails, and federal prisons. Prison is a hostile place, so don't come here at all.

Time

Time is a period the essential of all importance. Time is a period in which all things exist. In the Bible in the beginning when God created the heavens and earth. The Heaven and earth were said to be the first thing to be created in time.

Time is all we have on our hands whether you are free or locked up in a prison/jail cell confined. We all are serving time by merely existing. Those of us who are serving time in a prison or jail institution, no matter if we are innocent or guilty, we are where we are because we made a bad choice or decision somewhere in our lives.

Time is the nature of change. All things change with time, and yet nothing is extinguished. There is nothing in this world that is permanent. With time everything flows onwards, and all things are brought into being with the changing nature. Time and nature go hand and hand. They age themselves, glided in by constant movement, for still water will never reaches the sea.

Time is the existence of everything that happens in life. In a customary hour anything can transpire whether it be a miracle or a tragedy event. Time consists of seconds, minutes, hours, days, weeks, months, years, decades, and centuries. Time predicts one's experience during a particular period. Time is age, young or old.

Time on the clock keeps on ticking and ticking. Time is like a treasure every moment of our lives we share and strive to live out the duration of our ling pang. We should as human beings, Kings and Gods, the most magnificent creation, treasure every moment that we have, and treasure it more if you have someone special enough to spend your time with. And please remember that time waits for no one.

Yesterday is history, and tomorrow is a mystery. Today at this moment and point, time is considered a gift— that's why it's called the *present...*

Time can determine life or death. Time is loving, kind, hateful and mean. Everything consists of time.

In the book of Ecclesiastes in the Holy Bible Chapter 3:1-8 God words says,

> "1: To everything there is a season, and a time to every purpose under heaven. 2: A time to be born, and a time to die. A time to plant and a time to plunk up that which is planted. 3: A time to kill,

and a time to heal. A time to break down and a time to build up. 4: A time to weep and a time to laugh, a time to mourn and a time to rejoice. 5: A time to cast away stone, and a time to gather stones together. A time to embrace and a time to refrain from embracing. 6: A time to get and a time to lose, a time to keep and a time to cast away. 7: A time to reap and a time to sew, a time to keep and a time to cast away. 8: A time to love and a time to hate, a time for war and a time for peace..."

My question to the men and women that's incarcerated, how are you doing your time? I hope you are doing it by being productive and meaningful.

CHAPTER 11

Prisoner testimonies.

Mainstream society are you ready to peep into the minds of my fellow convicts who all have interesting stories to share about their confinement? If so, kick back, relax, and restrain yourself for this journey through the minds of men that have fallen victim to the system. Have you ever wondered how it felt to be incarcerated? To be locked out of a world you've been so accustomed to all your natural life? To be casted away because you made a few minor mistakes or broke the law once or twice in a society that itself was founded and built upon crime, and corruption.

America would rather lock away its citizens and breed criminals out of them than to seek prevention and rehabilitation programs to help deter people from re-offending.

Here and throughout this book you will hear stories, real stories of men I've met along my journey through the belly of the beast inside of this concrete jungle. 95% of these men are not animals as society and the system would want you to believe and like to label them as. These men are grandfathers, fathers, uncles, sons, brothers, cousins, nephews, and living human beings. These are some really great men, people just like you and me. Some are mentors, positive role models, motivational speakers, leaders, spiritual, college graduates, positive great men who unfortunately became unwilling casualties of the system. So, without further delay, let's read and hear what they have to say.

CHAPTER 12

Brother-A

In the name of Allah, the Beneficent, the most merciful, whom all praises are due.

My time is best spent while in prison here at Texarkana TX laying low and serving Allah, bowing down, submitting to do the will of Allah. This is what being a Muslim means.

I spend my time studying the Holy Quran and the Bible. After that last statement, I'm sure many of you are saying, "Whoa, Whoa, wait a minute, what did you just say, Brother-A? Did I hear you say the bible?"

A: Yes. I said Bible.

Q: But i thought you were a Muslim?"

A: Yes, I am. However, I follow Jesus too.

Q: Well, how could that be so?

A: Jesus' true religion was Islam, not Christianity. No disrespect to anyone's religion. I'm not here to debate or argue with anyone over this commentary statement, but the truth must be told. Christianity was a made-up religion. Jesus was a righteous good man, a prophet. He was killed and murdered for doing what Allah had put into him to do good deeds in Satan's world and they murdered him. I stand on this truth and am willing to challenge falsehood at any given moment, at the end of any given day, which is Allah's time. I bow down to my God Allah and submit to do his will. This is how I serve my time in this human warehouse called prison...

Wednesday, June 11, 2008

CHAPTER 13

Brother-B

    I'm from the city of Chicago, aka "Chi-Town", "Chiraq", or the "Windy City". I represent the Gangster Disciples (G.D.). I started gangbangin' at 10-years old. I've been shot three times, stabbed, and been to prison twice. My first bid was in the state prison system where I served 2.5 years. I got out for a year and went right back to the streets doing the same shit: gangbangin', robbing, selling drugs, and pimpin'. I'm now in federal prison on the West Coast serving time getting my weight up.

    I'll soon be released by the time these words in this book become manifested into publication. My great friend in the struggle and positive mentor Cashville has skillfully and marvelously structured together a real masterpiece. I've learned a great deal of wisdom and knowledge being in this brother presence. My time is best spent by taking advantage of every opportunity that comes before me.

    I've gotten my G.E.D. and have taken numerous

vocational trades since my incarceration: electrical, plumbing, construction, landscaping and air conditioning and heating. These trades are something that I will definitely take back out into society with me upon my release and I plan to apply them to my everyday life. I no longer have to feel that I'm just another product of my environment. I can apply myself now in the real world and have a real chance to strive and earn my own hard gained keeps. Ya' know what I mean!

I can start my own businesses and give out jobs to my people and deter them from going down the wrong path. I thank God for sparing my life. I died once on the operating table in the hospital and was announced dead for 1 minute and 25 seconds. However, God was not ready for me to go. God is amazing. God is the author of life and death. I also would like to give a special thanks and show my gratitude to the most Honorable Minister Mr. Louis Farrakhan of the Nation of Islam for teaching the lessons of life that his great teacher the Honorable Elijah Muhammed (whom all praise is due forever) taught before him.

The Honorable Minister Louis Farrakhan loves all of us. I thank God for this great fighter and warrior for standing up for all Black people. He's a real strong spiritual leader, a leader for justice, equality, freedom, and peace. He's ridiculed, envied, and hated on by many in the media because he stands on the principles of righteousness and isn't afraid to speak out against injustice. I learned to be a better person due to this great brother. The Honorable Elijah Muhammad left behind a brilliant giant with his teachings to help raise us up out of our unfit conditions America has put on us.

Well, to conclude this message and essay on how I spend my time while locked up in prison. I am more conscious and alive now after interacting with these great minded, intelligent individuals. I've been blessed during the course of my prison term. I'm now ready to face the world with my head held high and am confident in my abilities to succeed in life. Once again thank you Brother Cashville for being a positive influence on me, and for allowing me to be a part of this great project you're putting together for us Prisoners by giving us a chance to tell our stories. God Allah bless you Man!

CHAPTER 14

Brother-C

Prison time has woken me up. I say this because prison has exposed me to a whole other world. Before, I was mentally asleep and lost. My time now is spent learning as much as I can about myself, the world, different races of people, and the way this prison system operates. I'm basically in a university beyond bars right now. I exercise daily by lifting weights, running miles around the track, doing pull-ups, dips, and push-ups.

I try to stay physically and mentally fit. I like to read self-help motivational, inspirational, and exercise fitness books. I read the Bible and a lot of conscious literature as well to sharpen my thinking. It is a lot of sharp, wise, brilliant minds in here who have a wealth of knowledge. I like to pick the brains of the old heads too, or "O.G.'s" as we younger convicts like to call them. I learn things from the O.G.'s who've been in prison most of their lives. I listen and learn from them so that I can pick up off their experiences and not make the same mistakes they made.

One old head Brother, Cashville, an awesome swift-

thinking O.G. has taken me up under his wing since the beginning of my bid. He has taught me some very valuable life lessons. He is truthfully one bright, intelligent, and well-informed person when it comes to prison life. My brother Cashville has spent over 31-years of his life incarcerated, but has not let it break his spirits, He's nowhere near institutionalized and is real to the fullest on every level. He doesn't sugar coat shit. He'll tell you what it is and how it is. Cashville is a very humble and positive sole survivor. He's always extending out his hand to help a fellow convict who seeks his guidance or advice.

I have gotten my G.E.D and am taking various college courses to become a computer technician, as well as studying horticulture. I'd like to start farming on my family's land when I get out of prison. I want to grow and produce my own food consisting of healthy vegetables and fruits. Prison can be a very stressful experience, especially with a lot of idle time on your hands. It can destroy a person in so many ways if they succumb to the negativity and pitfalls that lie and waits for them.

My advice to anyone who's doing a prison bid, jail, or juvenile stretch is to utilize your time wisely. Time and life are precious. You only get one swing at the game of life, and one strikeout can take you out the game forever. Stop playing games with your life because once you pass on to the next life in the hereafter, ***it's a wrap!***

CHAPTER 15

<u>Brother-D</u>

Prison is a place the courts send a person to when they allegedly break the law and have been found guilty for committing a crime. Whether you are truly guilty or innocent, prison is where you are going to go once the court sentences you.

Myself, I was found guilty of selling crack cocaine and sentenced to 96-months in jail (8 years). While in prison I spent my time in the law-library fighting my case. It's 2007 now. Hopefully, when the two (2) point reduction pass on the disparity for the crack law changes, it will kick me straight out the front door with an immediately release. I already got 57-months in built up on my sentence. But in the meantime, and between time, while I'm here serving time, I'm going to continue bettering myself.

I am a school tutor in the education department in the prison school helping other prisoners like myself get their G.E.D! So far, I've helped six other prisoners achieve their G.E.D. Prison is what an individual makes of it. Either you're going to do the time wisely by rehabilitating yourself and learning how to be productive, or you can let the time do you. We as Black men must understand what we are doing to place ourselves in these unfortunate, high-risk situations when we pick up that sack or gun. We are taking penitentiary chances each day and there are serious penalties and consequences behind our actions.

My advice to all men who's facing jail or prison time is that while you are in there serving your time is to get your mind right and take full advantage of every opportunity to better yourself while you are incarcerated. and the goal is to come out better off than when you went in. Time waits for no one. Peace!

CHAPTER 16

<u>Brother-E</u>

I'm from Houston, Texas representing Tango Blast H-Town. I am serving 25-years for distribution of cocaine under the kingpin statue. As far as legal issues are concerned, I cannot elaborate into details about that. My case is still open and is being reviewed on my appeal, which I've been fighting in court now for years.

Besides fighting my case, I spend my time in prison as an artist. I like to draw portraits, tattoos, and wall paintings. I'm at beast—I can't be touched. My artistic gifts have allowed me to make very good money in prison. After coming to prison, I discovered that I could do many things, legally, that I had never taken the time out to do when I was in the free world. I was too busy making a bunch of money, running the streets engaging in all types of illegal activities.

I was hanging tough with the homies and having big fun with many beautiful women. I was partying and enjoying myself so much that never once could I see that I was about to be blindsided by the evil and severe consequences that lied ahead. I left my beautiful wife Lisa and my wonderful six kids out there alone in a cruel, cold-hearted world. Because of my criminal lifestyle I now sit here in a cage waiting on faith to prevail so that I can be set free. If that doesn't happen, then I'll have to do at least 15 more years behind bars.

My children are almost grown now. Their ages are 17, 16, 15, 14, 12, and 9. I have four boys and two girls. I'm blessed to have a strong, loyal, good wife to mother my kids. I'm also blessed that I left my family financially well off before I was separated from them. I was lucky to have legitimate businesses established that the feds could not legally confiscate from me like they did with a lot of my personal belongings. I don't say this to boast or brag because now amount of money is worth being separated from the presence of my family. I can only look forward to the weekend visits from my wife and kids,

That is what keeps me alive, inspired, motivated, and focused while I'm in prison. I've met many great men from other racial ethnic backgrounds that are positive good men

Prison can be a good or bad experience; it's basically what you make of it. I advise anyone who's reading this by saying this: **Crime is not worth giving up your freedom for**. So please make the right choices when you're taking risks in the streets...!

CHAPTER 17

Brother-F

What up doe.! Coming at y'all raw and live reppin' Detroit, Michigan. I'm locked down for a second and been gone for over three decades, but Ja' is good. I'm nearing release and I'm finna walk out those same swing doors that I came crawling through on my way in 28 years ago today. I can't wait to see some daylight and what's left of my beloved city Detroit. First and foremost, I got to thank and commend this good brotha I've known in this federal prison system for a few years now Ca$hville, for allowing me to be a part of this Fed Pain prison story adventure.

Boy, do I have prison life story ya dig. I salute tha' brotha for putting this prison story book together. It gives other prisoners a voice to be heard and a platform to stand on because us men in here have been shut out of mainstream society. We've basically been thrown away like yesterday trash by the federal government and the entire system.

It kills me to see so many young black men locked up for all these small-time crack and gun cases. It's ridiculous how the federal government is doing this. Their crimes should not even be considered a felony offense, their shit is state.

When I first came into the Federal Bureau of Prison {F.B.O.P.} back in 1988 for murder and kingpin heroin distribution it was a totally different prison setting. You didn't have small time crack dealers, crack addicts, pill-poppin', and petty gun/pistol charges in the federal system like you have now. You had mobsters, professional killers, racketeers, drug lords, and kingpin from every ghetto city in America.

You had drug cartels from throughout South American countries such as Nicaragua, Colombia, Costa Rica, and Mexico. All throughout the Caribbean, Cuba, Puerto Rico, Dominican Republic, Virgin Island, Jamaica, places like that, where they were smuggling tons and tons of pure cocaine, heroin, and marijuana by the ships and plane loads. Also, our U.S. Government officials were at the top of that criminal list too, truth be told.

So, I've spent my time here in these federal prisons by educating myself and the minds of these youngsters coming through those revolving prison doors. I'm teaching these young Black men knowledge about themselves and letting them know who they really are underneath the surface of their Black skin. I'm teaching them that they are the original Asiatic Black man. I've spent 28-years of my life schooling my young Afrikan brothers in here about their culture and history. Schooling them to what their ancestors went through as a people, kidnapped from their fucking homeland and brought over here to the northern shores of America in a strange land to be made slaves by wicked white Caucasian people who stripped and robbed them of their language, religion, names, culture, history and beliefs.

This is how I spend my time in wicked Babylon fighting the veils of the evil forces of Satan. It has been an ongoing uphill battle for me. Free Mumia Abu-Jamal and all other political prisoners trapped throughout America's prisons. The fight in the struggle for equality, justice, peace, and freedom will always continue to move forward.

Peace, one love Ja...Rastafarian!

CHAPTER 18

<u>Brother-X</u>

Greetings and peace everyone who's reading this book. I'm Brother-X and I'm representing D.C., the nation's capital. First and foremost, I would like to thank Allah and then give thanks to my brother in this struggle for freedom and justice. I want to thank him for bringing his idea to my attention and offering me a chance to be a part of this great book by sharing my story. Since I met and over the years I've known this magnificent great brother, he's always shown great character presenting himself as a respectful, humble and honorable man, who carries the Afrikan spirit around inside of him that spells, peace, and unity, for all humanity.

Currently, I am serving a 12-year bid, but by the time this book is put out into publication I hope to be free and released from prison. I spend my time while incarcerated educating myself and working out daily. I have been in all types of physical altercations: battles, knife fights, so forth and so on in the first few years of my bid. I've been stabbed three separate times since I've been locked up, and each time I've almost died. Each incident was a different situation, but each scenario particularly the same: something small and petty.

For those of you that don't know about us "D.C. prisoners" we have a bad reputation in the F.B.O.P. This is mainly due to us not having a state prison system. Lorton, the former state prison we did have, is now closed. Every crime in D.C. is considered a federal offense bid in the federal prison system. That's why there are so many of us in F.B.O.P. But nevertheless, we all are being systematically oppressed and railroaded in these white folks' court rooms.

While I exercise and read, I also spend my time networking, multi-tasking on a non-geographical scale. I'm trying to bridge the gap between all the geographical division bickering amongst us Black men. As a race of people here in the United "Snakes" of America, I'm doing everything in my power to unify us Black men so that we can come together collectively as a race and create a solid unity among us. I remember the first Million Man March I attended in Washington D.C.

That day I was high on that "boat", which is known as "PCP". I was so gone I didn't have a clue as to what was going on. My cousin Snake told me to go home, clean up, take a bath, and meet him at his house in two hours. I asked slim, what was going on? How come all those Black folks gathering up on the

Washington Mall? My cousin hipped me that the Honorable Minister Louis Farrakhan from the Nation of Islam had called for a Million-Man March.

After I went home and took a shower my high had come down. I got fresh and clean and put on a silk, white suit. My cousin and I walked eight blocks and became engulfed in a of sea of nothing but Black men. The Million Man March was the most electrifying experience of my life. After the closing end of the Million-Man March, a week later my cousin and I joined the ranks of the Nation of Islam. Ever since that day in 1995, we have been submitting to do the will of Allah. I am a student minister, and a fruit of the Nation of Islam.

I educate and teach Black men how to be themselves, how to love their own people, and let them know that they have the ability to grow into the likeness of God Allah if they are willing to clean their lives up. The Honorable Elijah Muhammad teaches us that we have to do for ourselves, honor and love ourselves and our women and children. We must come into the wisdom of knowledge, know who our true enemies are, and we must separate from the slave master's children. Islam is for peace. We don't teach hate; we teach love and the truth to our people. As Salaam Alaikum...!

CHAPTER 19

Brother-H

I am from China. Currently, I'm in the United States Federal Prison for money laundering and tax evasion. I want to talk to you about "Chi" and prison life from my experience. Chi is the energy of life force that we all have within us. Some of us as Chinese people believe an imbalance of chi is what causes illness. Chi has a variety of functions, but its primary duty is to be fuel that harmonizes the body. This understanding is what helps me get through my period of incarceration.

The Chinese way is like other Asian cultures in that we emphasize balance and moderation. You can benefit from this philosophy if you honor the chi that is within you by taking care of your mind, body, and spirit to maintain balance. Let's eat properly, exercise moderately, get plenty of rest, and keep ourselves emotionally stable. I live in balance and harmony and let the time do itself, trusting in the chi.

Have you ever worried whether there would be enough air to breathe? How often do you ponder what you would do if the laws of gravity ceased to operate? For some reason, you never worry about the very essential elements you need to stay alive. Chi, you just trust they will be there, and they are.

Chi, you trust that your heart will beat, your blood will flow, your lungs will expand, and that you will stay firmly planted on this earth. Chi, you trust that every organ within you will do exactly as it should. Chi, you trust that your body will support you. Why not extend that trust to every area of your life. Trust chi that the universe and creator will provide everything that you need without any effect on your part. All you need to do is ask and trust. We can honestly acknowledge the wrong we have done and if possible, fix it. If it's not possible to repair the damage, we can learn from the mistakes, so we don't repeat it.

Guilt isn't a pleasant emotion, but it is a sign of a healthy psyche. I acknowledge my errors while being locked up in prison, willingly knowing chi that I am a lovable, worthwhile person. I live in balance and harmony—chi...!

CHAPTER 20

Brother-Z

I'm from Seattle, Washington. My time best spent while incarcerated is rebuilding my life. Coming to prison, I was lost out there in the free world society. I was living a reckless and dangerous criminal lifestyle, which has now gotten me serving a 360-month (30-year) prison sentence. I am in federal prison for distribution of meth. I ran two meth labs and sold a lot of meth out of it. I know this is a Caucasian drug of choice, but where I live at in Seattle, the money was fast and good when it came to selling this product. I made plenty of money peddling meth, but it wasn't worth 360-month sentence I now have.

A life was taken and lost in my meth dealings and it caused this precious young lady's life to be stolen from her family. I regret ever knowing what methamphetamine was now that I sit here in prison with plenty of time on my hands to reflect back over my life in the past.

During my experience dealing with drugs, I felt like

I was playing a winning game of chess with the devil. However, even with his queen and both rooks off the board, I still didn't stand a chance in this wicked game because this is Satan's world. After being locked up in this federal prison system around all types of different prisoners, people from all over the world and hearing a lot of their life stories, I have come to realize that the devil has a lot of power to rule over us. He makes you feel like you're winning and that you're powerful, all the while he's tricking you to lead a life of crime instead of doing what's right.

I met Cashville while I was incarcerated. I have never met a person like this brother. When I first heard his story, about his struggle and all the years he's been locked up in prison and the positive changes he has made, it inspired me to make that same sacrifice and do positive work too. Cashville taught me a lot just by being in his presence day-in and day-out. One can't do nothing but tip their hat off to Cashville and admire, love, and respect this humble, fearless, and knowledgeable Souljah. He's one helluva book author and has an extraordinary Way of sharing knowledge and telling his story.

I appreciate him for giving me advice and the jewels he dropped on me along the way. I really appreciate him helping me on my 2241-Motion and helping me to get back into the courts to give 360-months back off of my sentence. He pointed out the legal errors that my court appointed attorney made and should have known better about. He pointed out how the court enhanced my sentence illegally. It took me three and a half years to get back in, but the courts are finally correcting the errors they made with my case.

If I hadn't met Cashville when I did, I probably would have never discovered the legal errors the courts made. When you're in the white man's courtroom they mess us over real bad. Ain't no such a thing as "Justice for a Black person in the United 'Snakes' of America. I'm forever indebted to Cashville. He has a free spirit out of this world that's like no other person I've met in here. He practically saved my life. I honor and respect the big homie.

My advice to anyone who's reading this great book, especially if you are locked up doing a long stretch is to get in that law-library and try to find that needle in the haystack because that's the key that will set you free...Peace and much luv!

CHAPTER 21

Brother-Dollar

Dollar be my name, tricking a ho out her money be my game... ha... ha... ha. I'm from the M-Town reppin' Memphis 10. I'm serving time for selling that hard, which is Cocaine. I'm from South Memphis off Trigg & Lauderdale. I was a product of my environment. My family and I we grew up dirt poor as hell. My daddy was a pimp, lost somewhere in the streets, penitentiary or cemetery. Hell, I don't know where he is, I never met the bastard. I had to take on the father role in my household and take care of my other two brothers and sister.

Since I was the oldest, I had to step up to the plate, get out there on the block and get it how I live—you hear me. It's a lot of young niggas in these penitentiaries because they had to grow up fast and be the man of the house. To protect and provide they had to turn to the streets, selling drugs or whatever crime there was to turn to. It's a cold world we live in. Ain't no good jobs out there for a young unskilled Black man and woman, so we have to get in where we fit-in and get it out the mud. Ain't nobody damn sho' putting it in yo' hand unless it's a sack or gun. Like Boosie Badass said, "I was taught to be a man".

Well, getting to the point at hand, my time spent while here in prison is looking for new avenues and alternatives to learn how to make an honest living once I get back out of prison, which is very soon. Thanks to President Obama for changing the disparity in the crack law 18-to-one that put me from 120 months to 84 months. The 2-point level reduction. I have 6-years in and am waiting for a letter as we speak right from the courts with my immediate release.

I have also taken the time out to get my Barber's license too while I was in prison. I plan to work in my cousin's barber shop once I get out. If that doesn't do well, my backup plan is to go into computer tech. I can also rap and write music. So, Prison wasn't a bad thing after all. It actually saved my life because before when I was out, I was getting shot and hit up several times. I'm still here by the grace of God. God is good. A merciful Good. So, in closing, I want to thank Cashville, the big homie for allowing me to be able to tell my story. A wise and intelligent man. Shout to all my niggas out there holding it down... You hear me...!

CHAPTER 22

Brother- Freeway

I go by the name of Freeway. After a while in prison, I made the conscious decision that I would no longer be a victim no matter what type of situation I was in. I will always look for a way to win. After a lot of reading and studying, I learned that there were two sides to every coin and the sunny day starts right after the darkness of night. That means that if you can withstand the worst that's been thrown at you, then the fight is going to get easier. Too many people lay down at the first sign of an obstacle. It's like everyone has courage until it is tested and challenged. Coming into jail can be one of the greatest challenges a person could ever face.

I've seen prison breakdown some of the strongest, baddest, and toughest men that I've known. I've seen men turn to other men for comfort and for protection. I've seen weak men that would rather die than face another day in jail. They cut their wrists, hang themselves, overdose on pills, and any other type of crazy act to take their own lives. I learned a long time ago that I had to be strong, and that the race is not won by the swift and quick but rather by those who endure to the end.

My teacher and father told me to give up every limb of your body but save the brain for last. What he meant was that the mind or brain is the most important possession that a man has. He used to say that in church have (God) in your heart, but also have Him in your mind, too. I personally feel that I am the greatest man alive and that I was created in the image of God. I'm one of the greatest creations that Mother Nature has ever created. I have the power to make things the way that I want them to be. I'm not a helpless being in this world. I can control my environment, but first, I must have to have control over myself.

I had to learn that I was a weak person with many desires that needed filling and those desires have led me sitting right here in prison. Once I came to grips with my situation my mind immediately began to search for opportunities. I've always felt that my life is the most important life that ever lived and that I would make a difference in the world. I don't want my legacy to be just that of a Black man convicted of selling cocaine. There's much, much more to Freeway that meets the eyes and ears.

I genuinely love people. I hate to see people hurting or in need. I think America is the greatest place to live. I don't agree with the stiff drug laws and the severity of the punishment that the law gives out to people. I think there's a lot of corrupt people in power, but there's no system that's perfect. If you don't like the way the system is set up, you have every right to take power in your hands. Go to congress in Washington D.C. and plead your case.

I have no problem going head-to-head with no man or woman. See, I've been living in the fire for seventeen and a half calendar years in the belly of the beast, and I think I'm starting to enjoy it. It has all became one big challenge to me. I will keep my spirits high and won't stop until I break out of these walls. I will never let the "Institution" break my will and make me forget that I'm "the Real Freeway". Don't get me wrong, I play the role, speak, and smile, and even pretend that I want another chance when I'm caught breaking an institution rule. But in all actuality, there's nothing else they can do to me or take from me. What I have locked into my mind, the way I think, can't be stopped,

I can see myself standing on top of the mountain top. I saw Martin Luther King Jr. dream, and I've started to share with others what would they do with an army of brother's who think like me or even just two or three. I started to make a lot of sacrifices. Once I became a man, I gave up childish things like toys. What do I consider toys? A toy is anything that takes a man's mind off of his mission and distracts him from reality.

Most people look for an easy route and way to avoid real struggle. What they do is put their minds to sleep by listening to trash radio, watching T.V., reading those garbage gangster or sex books, and just overall playing around. What most people don't realize is that if we give our mind a problem—any problem—it will figure out a way to solve it. We must be the "king" of our dome.

I want to grow wealthy and healthy. Those are my goals in life. I now have a reason to live. I used to not care whether I lived, died, or ended up in prison. Now I dream about going home and raising little Black Gods & Goddesses. I learn something every day. I read the Wall Street Journal and other prominent publications to keep in touch with the outside world. There is nothing new under the sun. All we have to do is put our own twist-on-it and present it to the world in our own way. I've also learned to use other people's mind, body, and resources... Freeway!

CHAPTER 23

<u>Brother-I</u>

This is how I feel about being locked up in federal prison. First and foremost, I committed the crime, I broke the law, and I knew that if you did the crime, you've got to do the time, straight up and down. The way I feel about being in prison is a feeling that is hard to put on paper. Before I even get into this, I would like to talk about family and friends. I feel like I have been forgotten about. I thought that I had love on the streets after all the work that I put in. Although I wasn't necessarily the top dawg, I made sure that I took care of my family and friends.

However, since I've been in prison, I've only received three letters from one of my homeboys in all of my three years. I can count on one hand the amount of outside contact I've received from people. And the money I've received from a few people I am grateful for. But it's still not enough to cover the $147.00 fine the prison has put on my books.

One thing about prison is that no matter where you

go, the guards will always be on a power trip. They will talk to you any type of way, like you are lower than dirt. These crackers are some of the most disrespectful men and women I have ever met. One of the worst things they can do to you—which also seems to be their favorite—is they love to tear through your personal mail and all of your personal belongings.

Prison is all about control. They have some of the smallest and pettiest rules here that you must abide by. A lot of what us prisoners face behind these walls is projection from the guards. A lot of these C.O.'s actually get bullied around in their personal lives outside of work. They then come back to work and take it out on us inmates. A lot of guards will entice and try to provoke us to do something to them so that we can give them a reason to act in an inappropriate fashion or disrespectful manner toward us.

They will take every inch of an opportunity to downgrade you, or physically hurt you in every legal or illegal way possible. They know we can't retaliate or risk getting another charge on our sentence. What's also crazy is that the world expects us inmates to respect them and other law enforcement and to come out of this prison "rehabilitated". How can a man with such an attitude, such anger and hatred built up inside them come through? It's not possible, but it's going to take a lot of patience.

Truth is, there is part of me that agrees with the prison system when it comes to a cold-blooded serial *killer, rapists, and child molester. These types of people need stiff sentences and deserve hard time. It's crazy the amount of time they give someone just for selling drugs like crack and cocaine.*

Personally, I think there should be some changes in the way that prison time is given out. I don't like prison and will never return...!

CHAPTER 24

__Brother-Bo__

This is my experience in prison and how I feel about it. Being locked up has it's negative and positive effects to it. A lot of us know about the negatives of this life, so I'll spend my time talking about the positive. Prison gives a lot of us time to think and reflect after we've been slowly killing ourselves on the outside. We can now see that they we were living in hell, mentally destroying ourselves and using drugs, alcohol, and cigarettes etc. You now stop those bad habits and get the time you need to gain back self-control and your natural health.

You can use your time and place in prison as an institution of higher learning instead of just doing time. You can develop and improve your conditions and skills intellectually. You also educate yourself more and learn some life-long lessons. You can network with other conscious-minded brothers and learn from their mistakes. You can truly change for the best and come into the reality of who you really are and what you were meant to be while in prison.

Take full advantage of the time and opportunities you have while in prison and capitalize off it positively, physically, mentally, financially, and most importantly spiritually. We can't do nothing without God's permission, and that transcends whatever religion you ascribe to. Peace!

CHAPTER 25

Brother Somali

A good brother from Somali... In his Somali language.

Uveedo Soring xusuus koban anisso ah jay laani Cl Raxman awCal waxoon hal kan kuxu saayoo aRin Tan aan hada u8u xlr nahay amerika horay in laanan bur cada Kuburin waxoonoha Far soma yagaan waxoona keshafoyn Jirey war shod kutaal Somalie Goor ahaan MaGoolade Bossaso waxaan hel kaas ka sha fana yey mudo jhan sanodo

Kadib mar kll shafadll layga eRyey waxoon latashaday dholin yaro ashoo xlbadey waxay na lGula taliyeen inaan 'yaGa kamid nofdo P kadihna woon kubll Ray kadib h. Shus keya Gii xumoo waxoon ka am ba box ney MoGoolada GoRoGd toe Rn kh dn koonumaRay neWaxunna nopsoogub Blyey America

y bad waynta hin dia meel GereCed utlRta 7200 oo may! ayeenaRaG noy MoRkob Mar kll aan weeRa Ray Mor kab kll waxoona dhex goley xaRoobi

Kadibna wenna fob tey

OOan hodo ku xlr na hey
God bay!

CHAPTER 26

Caucasian-J

Being locked up has taught me respect for the law. Having been through the state system and the federal prison system, I now know just how crooked the system is. From your defense lawyer (whose first responsibility is to the court), to the judge, all the way down to the officers that the taxpayers pay to "care" for us prisoners. I want to state for the record, I am Caucasian/European. This book my fellow prisoner friend Cashville is presenting to society is not about race, so the stories you are reading in this book are based on personal individual's real-life experiences. Stories of people like myself who's white and a victim of the system. I understand that it is easier to obey the laws of this country than it is to become involved once more in a system that is driven by hatred, motivated by money, and possessed by power...!

CHAPTER 27

Brother-K

I'm from Nashville, Tennessee. I think being locked up gives a man time to find his or herself if they are doing wrong. He also finds out which family and friends really cared for him. Since I was a businessman, you find out who was there just for business and who really cared for you personally. Best advice I can tell a person is be careful what business you go into. And one other wise advice is watch your friends because they will change on you, turn on you, and betray you if you aren't careful.

CHAPTER 28

Brother-L

Being locked up has taught me a very valuable lesson. There are some things that I have learned being here that I would have never learned if I stayed on the streets. I learned pretty quickly who my friends were and who they weren't. Prison has shown me that I'm the one has to change my old ways and to accept responsibility for my own actions. I used to think it was everyone else's fault that I was here in this predicament. I realize now that one has to change his negative into a positive and learn from other people's mistakes as well as my own.

Since I've been incarcerated, I have accomplished a lot of self-control. I used to have bad habits using drugs, drinking alcohol, gambling, and being addicted to sex. Since I've been in prison, I have gotten rid of all those bad vices. I no longer have those desires I just mentioned. Four years of being in prison has really helped me to change my behavior a lot. I advise anyone who's reading this book not to risk their freedom for a life of crime. Ain't nothing in this world worth losing your life or freedom for unless your hand is forced, and you have to defend yourself or protect your family and loved ones. I personally will never ever sell drugs again. The money might be good while its coming in fast, but it's not worth the time and your freedom you will be paying for that rush. That's all I gotta say. Don't get caught and locked up. Stay out of jail and prison...Peace Out!

CHAPTER 29

Baby-B

Words spoken by "Baby-B". Sup, I'm from Durham, N.C. Here's my story: At age 9 years old I was introduced to the Gang lifestyle. "Fattz" was the big homie that I looked up too. He didn't want me in the streets at all. He was a positive role model for me. Fattz always told me to go to school, make good grades, and play sports. If I got caught skipping school or doing bad things in the neighborhood, Fattz would make two other older kids fight me. He made sure that the older kids didn't stomp me out or beat me too bad. He just wanted them to do enough to get the lesson through to my head—literally.

But the other big homie "West" was a different breed of a man. He was the negative force that played a major role in my gang involvement. West would encourage me to rock my hood colors and taught me how to throw up my gang signs and rep my set. West would also push me to go to school, but not as much as Fattz did. West gave me my nickname "Baby B" because I was the youngest out of the whole hood.

West and Fattz were always in disagreement about me. I wanted to be up under Fattz, but he didn't want me to gangbang. West wanted me to be down with him, but I didn't wanna bang his set "Rollin' 30's". So, I went outside the hood and found a set from Compton, California known as the Eastside Kelly Park Compton Crips.

As I got older and time went on, I caught a lot of beef from Bloods sets and other Crips sets. My name really started to ring because I was known to be young and wild, even though if you were to meet me you would say I was laid back and calm. I started traveling to other cities and states in the country like Raleigh N.C.; Chapel Hill, N.C.; Orlando, F.L.; Philadelphia, Pennsylvania. Eventually, I started getting charges one after the other on my record.

I caught an attempted murder case in Durham N.C. that forced me to stay in the county for a while. That case ended up with me on probation and on house arrest. I then caught a fed case for having a gun. My first time ever going to a U.S.P. Prison, was at 23 years old. My time here at this U.S.P. has been extremely boring and depressing. Everyone around me is miserable and doing football numbers. Violence can occur over anything, and it's usually over the smallest things: skipping line over the telephone, using someone's computer, or simply being from the wrong neighborhood.

So to be smart and wise, I pretty much stay to

myself, mind my own business, and stay in my own lane. My main focus and goal are getting out of prison and going home to my kids. One of my homies encouraged me to take some classes. I'm in a few vocational courses and the (RDAP) which means the Residential Drug Abuse Program. Through these two experiences I've learned that prison is more of a mindstate than a physical trap. A person has to dig deep to find that inner desire for change.

I don't look at my situation as a failure or a minus. I look at it as a plus. I say this because the lifestyle I was living in the streets was reckless. Things could've been much worse for me had I not ended up in prison. I could've lost my life, or worse, taken the life of someone else. I thank God that I only received 34 months in federal prison instead of more time than I can process. My advice to the youth is: "stay in school, get your education, and cherish freedom...!"

CHAPTER 30

Brother Black

Alright, here's my story. First and foremost, I am currently incarcerated in Federal Prison serving 63 months for being a convicted felon in possession of a firearm. I'm a country boy straight off the farm in Alabama, and I rep the city of Talladega. My life of crime started in the year of 1999, when I was first exposed to the streets. I was 11 years old then. I was hooked on weed real heavy, but I was always broke. At that age, I didn't have no hustle about myself, so I tried to take the easy way out by shoplifting to support my habit.

Eventually, things got even worse. I started robbing and carjacking to support my habit. That is until the undercover officers started locking me up and sending me to boot camps, detention centers, group homes, and drug rehabs. Even after all that I continued to do wrong when I got out. I was the very definition of insanity: doing the same shit but expecting different results each time.

The year of 2007 is when I first met the love of my life, my daughter's mother. In August she was pregnant with our daughter. Sadly, I went to state prison in November of 2007 and had to do 13 months. When I got out in December of 2008, my little girl was 7 months. Well, the drugs still took over my life and I left my family again in June 2009 in December again, and have been gone ever since. I was exactly like my father and following in his footsteps.

My Dad was in and out of prison himself. How was he going to teach me right from wrong, or show me things in life when he didn't know anything about life either? My prison is located in Mississippi somewhere. But "God Allah" has blessed me to get out in 2018 and get another chance at life. Most of all importantly, I've got another chance to raise up my daughter who needs me to teach her the right way of life itself. I can't thank her mom enough for the amazing job she's done in raising her while I've been gone.

My whole entire prison experience has really opened my eyes and made me see things from a different perspective. I'm changing and am now being more responsible for myself. For so long I was caught up chasing a dollar bill in the foolish ways I was, not knowing that "Allah God" is the best knower of all things. He had a plan for me that I couldn't see. I was running around in those streets chasing a high so much that he had to sit me down one last time to get my attention.

As I sat and reflected, I found my natural talents. I discovered that I'm good at drawing, cutting hair, and *numerous other things. I can actually make a legitimate livelihood once I get out of prison. I don't have to sell drugs, steal, rob, or kill to take care of my family. I'm going to challenge my abilities to do things for myself. I want to open up my own barber shop and draw artwork. In closing my story, I can't end this writing without mentioning my mentor in here in this university behind bars we call prison: Cashville. Give him thanks for allowing me to share my life and prison experience. I'm using my time learning, studying, and educating myself from all schools of thoughts. The mind is a terrible thing to waste, so don't waste yours.*

CHAPTER 31

Brother-M

I am a former kingpin drug dealer out of Florida. The United States Federal Government hates it when a Black man can make millions of untaxed dollars. The U.S. Government feds came and took me off the streets at an early age. I was 24 years old at that time, on my way to USP located in the mountains. This was a very overrated and hostile federal prison, not a place for a boss like me to be locked up at. The federal prison system ain't nothing like it was in the mob day.

However, I can say I have met famous people like T.I, the rapper Gucci mane, some Mexican drug cartel members, and all other types of big-time criminals. Don't get it wrong, it is very high profile in some areas, but I can say this system is overrated. You live and you learn. Some men in here use their time wisely and some people are lost, in denial, and just simply can't get right.

One thing I can say from personal experience is that the best ideal and plans can be developed from right here behind these walls. But a lot of these guys in this pen act like they don't believe in themselves. Always remember this: it doesn't take special powers to come up with a master plan for yourself. Decide what you want and list out everything you have to do to get there. Then, one by one, cross those things off your list until you've reached your goal. Peace!

9-2-2015!

CHAPTER 32

Brother-Migo

In 2004, I was barely old enough to be in the county jail. I was 17-years old and didn't know what to expect. I was arrested and taken to the Carrizales-Rucker Detention Center in Olmito, Texas. This was one of the most vicious jails in the Southern District of Texas and home of the "Vallucos", a well-known and respected Hispanic gang. While at the booking area, I was stripped down to nothing then received my county jail issue. I was then thrown in a large room with a lot of different people.

I was immediately approached by the T.S. Texas Syndicate gang member and they asked me "who I was riding with?" Of course, at the time I was not "riding" with nobody. Riding in jail or prison means what gang you belong to. After a few questions, the man left me alone and I looked for an empty spot in the room to lay and sleep. I did not find one. I had to sit-up and fall asleep sitting down. Early in the next morning around 4:00am the guard woke everyone up.

We had to turn in our blankets to be able to eat breakfast. "No blanket, no breakfast!" he kept yelling.

I was taken to population later that night. I was placed in B-Block with all the "Vallucos Members". The Valluco members quickly approached me again. I was asked a million questions about any kind of affiliation I might have. I was told that if they found out I was lying about running with someone I was going to regret it and be sorry. After the talk with the "Capataz", which is the person running the block, I had to talk to one other person running the block too. He was known as "The Talachero", the person responsible for laying down all the rules of the house to me.

He let me know that Rule #1 was to "Talacha", which means clean in slang. I had to do this for 5-days in a row, and I couldn't pay no one else to do it for me even if I had money. Money can't always solve your problems in jail. Actually, it can create more problems for you. After I did the "Talacha" for the 5-days, I was told to lay back and I was allowed to watch "El Tubo" which means T.V. during the morning hours of the day. I violated a few rules one morning. I flushed the "Yoga" (toilet) and took a piss while everyone was having breakfast. At the time, I didn't know any better. I was green and fresh in jail.

"The Capataz" asked to talk to me and he was pissed. He asked me if I knew the rule I had broken. Honestly, I didn't know. I was explained by the "talachero" all the rules, but I did not pay too much attention to him. I was let off the hook with my luck with minor things that I had to do. After 11-months in county jail I was released. I was 19-years old. I lasted 5-years in the streets before I was arrested again at age 24. This time I went through the same jail, then state prison at a correctional facility known as T.D.O.I.

I was already riding with the Vallucos, so I didn't have it hard no more. Just the basic rules, respect and stay out of trouble. Pay your bills and don't run up no debts. Don't get nothing over what you have on your books. Serious consequences will be applied if any of the prison or jail house rules are violated or disrespected. I was released at age 25, again after 11-months. I stayed out for 6 and a half months and then I picked up a federal indictment. I was sentenced to 8-years and 1-month. I've been in 8 and a half years now.

My advice to anyone is to stay out of trouble. Prison is not a place you want to be at. Everyday you're told what to do from these punk ass C.O.'s who decide when you eat and when you have to lock down. Everything in the U.S.P. Penitentiary here at Big Sandy is controlled, especially movements. I'm currently taking the drug rehab program and awaiting to be released early. I ask God to please help me and not to ever let me fall into this hell ever again. Valluco 100% Brownsville, Texas L.A. Southmost. Oh yeah, when you are locked up you find out quick who your true *friends are and who really loves you. Keep your nose clean.*

7-28-2015

CHAPTER 33

Brother-L.C.

I'm from Chicago, Illinois, and here's my story. I grew up on the Westside and became a part of an organization known as the "Four Corner Hustlers". The organization is where I looked for love, support, and financial opportunity. I received all that and much more from this organization. However, I have to ask myself was it worth all the pain I put my family through? The answer is No! The street life ain't never been fair: the drugs, the violence, the jails. The system is injustice; it's not for us, or by us!

Your so-called friends will turn their backs on you for the system. They say they're doing it to help justice prevail, or are they getting paid in some other way? You got people that are referred to as paid informants. These are men and women who could manufacture a story as quickly as you could recite your phone number. I've learned that inmates in federal holding facilities routinely buy sell and steal narcotics, concoct testimonies, and then share their perjury with federal authorities in exchange for a reduction in their sentence.

Often these inmates testify against people they've never met before and corroborate on crimes they've never even witnessed. They lie with no regard and often with the government's blessings. They are modern-day slave catchers in the inhumane brutalization of Black people. These federal agents and prosecutors have been accused of helping move the scheme along and in most cases, they provide convicts with information in order to help them fabricate their lies. How can you build a case against someone filled with lies?

I myself have been in and out of the system half of my life. Like so many young Black men that find themselves trapped in America's penal system I was determined to find a way out, so I reverted to my old ways. They say one of the most dangerous things they can do is lock a man up and for him to have nothing to do all day. But it was in this exact situation that I found "Allah" in my cell. Holding cells are like Chicago train stations, but worse. You get in where you fit in.

You got dudes sprawled out on the pissy floor, sitting on steel toilet stools and hard benches, as well as sleeping under them. The clamor of loud voices is maddening. It's like listening to everyone screaming at the same time. Guys lie for nothing. We be in them cells, waiting to hear our names called as if "Allah" Himself were standing at the door choosing who will make it into the Gates of Heaven.

In jail, lawyers are like Gods that work for the devil, only worse considering a prisoner is dependent on them as the intermediate. That's where the problem starts. It's like being in a foreign country and you don't know how to speak the language. Many men have signed their names on the dotted lines, paying the lawyer a lot of money hoping he will secure his freedom. Lawyers are some of the biggest crooks ever that "Allah" created.

Over half the federal system is full of informants, snitches who are eager for a free ticket out of jail. In the feds they have an old saying: "you got two kinds of people—the ones that told, and the ones who wish they had told!" Those that told will never stop telling even for the sake of their own moral integrity. Those that don't staunchly refuse to compromise their code of honor and ethics because it's the very essence of who they are. Real men do not tell on their friends, family members, wives, or kids. They would rather die for what they believe in.

Opportunity does not go away; it just goes to someone else. I'm working on becoming a better man, so I'm doing my time constructively. I want to be an asset to myself, my community, and my family as a whole. Even though the shackles ain't on our feet anymore we are still mentally enslaved until we find out who we are and what our purpose is here on earth. We have to wake up soon.

I'd like to thank My guy Cashville for giving me this

golden opportunity to share my story. I'd also like to give praise to the prophet Noble Drew Ali, to whom all praises due forever. I'd like to give praises to the best knower and guide in the person of Master Fard Muhammad (to whom all praises due forever). I'll also would like to give praises to The Honorable Elijah Muhammad (to whom all praises are due forever). And last but not certainly least, I'd like to give praises to The Honorable Minister Louis Farrakhan, who is in our mist today leading and guiding the way!..

CHAPTER 34

__Brother-Youngman__

Today is July 24, 2015 and my name is Youngman. I'm a 47-year old Native American from Mescalero, N.M. I am Apache and a federal inmate in a U.S.P. I am thankful for my friend and fellow prisoner Cashville for allowing me to share my story, So here it is...

Right off the Rip, I think the United Snakes Government are a bunch of egotistical bureaucrats, subhuman mongrels, flesh and metal eating, human waste eating parasites...heathens to a certain extent. I don't know and I don't care if they believe in how a person is to be judged, but I know that when a person dies he is judged by his work's, so faith without works is dead. One day they'll have to stand tall before God and he'll judge them by their works. If their names aren't written in the Lamb's book of life, it's straight to Hell you go!!

There are five stages of Hell. 1)The burning lake of fire and sulfur. 2) Brimstone, 3) Hades. 4)SHEOL. 5) Hell. Each stage is more painful than the next, more *suffering and then, there's Hell where the devil, Satan himself will torture you day and night forever and ever. No sleep, no rest, just TORTURE!!! So, it sucks to be with a guilty conscience if you have one. And, if they don't like what I'm saying I'm only exercising my 1st amendment constitutional right: freedom of speech.*

Everything for me started in 2012, when I was arrested on my tribal Land for A&B (assault and battery). I went to tribal court, did jail time, probation, and paid fines for my assault and battery crime. 1.5 years later I did another assault and battery on my Rezz. This time the Feds filed charges against me, and I ended up in federal court. The initial charges against me were dropped due to the fact that the feds were not consistent with their paperwork. The federal judge said it was all inappropriate!!! I should have been released!!! But to justify my incarceration the feds bought up my old charge of A and B (Assault and battery) in 2012, which I've already paid my dues for.

They said it's not "Double Jeopardy" due to the fact of Jurisdictional reason? But the constitution that governs this land states that "No person should be subjected to a second punishment for the same act or crime, of life or limb". I believe the united Snakes government is the Pimp and the FBI agents are the bitches, out to fuck us criminals in the feds game of life. I feel betrayed by the ones we've trusted and elected into office, because authority figures are supposed to make things, right?

Now, my life in prison is a life of uncertain, unpredictable journeys. The atmosphere here is a violent one. You have to beware of your surroundings at all times. Don't get caught slipping or you could get filled full of holes and end up "DEAD"!!! Prison life is all about survival man.

I'm now 55-days away from the door on a 38-month prison term. I will make sure that my life on the outside will be one of rational thinking and filled with positive outcomes. I'm going to start doing the good things in life: like going to church with my family, visiting old friends, and staying SOBER.

Lastly, I don't want you to look at me as a terrorist or criminal. I'm just a product of the system, a CORRUPT system, and that's my story. Resentment=none; Resentful=nope; Remorseful=A little; Grateful= yeah!!!

THE END.

CHAPTER 35

I believe that the challenge of every prisoner is to know how to survive prison tactics and remain intact. The goal is to emerge from prison undiminished, and to conserve and even replenish your own beliefs. Your first objective is to learn the convict rules and codes of conduct in any imprisonment setting. You have the prison authority rules and regulations that you must abide by, and then you have some strict and serious convict rules to go by. These are the 5-basic rules that all prisoners must adhere to. Breaking or violating any of these rules can result in some serious repercussions and consequences. The survival rules are as follows...

Rule 1: Respect. Respect is a must. In order to get respect, one has to give respect. Do not disrespect anyone, unless you are ready to kill, or be killed about it. Rule 2: NO Snitching. Telling or ratting on someone in jail is a big no-no. Even the prison administration officials don't even like "Rats". They will use you for information on your fellow prisoners and then set you out to the rest of the prisoners once they get tired of using you. They will let the entire population know that you are or once did work for them.

Don't ever allow the title of a "rat" to become attached to your name. That can get you filled with holes in your body ASAP. Also, don't ever talk to the prison officials or the administration, S.I.S., and any other type of agent by yourself. Always have another person/prisoner with you. This way you can't be falsely accused of Ratting or working with the administration. A solid, stand-up convict will always cover his ass when the prison officials want to talk with him about anything concerning a situation. No matter what that situation pertains too never play with the Police/C.O.'s, they're not your friends.

Rule 3: Mind Your Own Business. That means stay out of other people's way and keep to yourself. Hear no evil, see no evil, and speak no evil. Stay in your lane. Rule 4: No Stealing. No one likes a thief, not even other thieves. Don't touch anything that does not belong to you. Keep your dick beaters to yourself. And last, but not least Rule 5: Homosexuality. Now don't get it twisted. People have their sexual preference and that's cool. I have no problem with that. I don't knock what another man does, even if I don't condone it myself. But it is what it is, especially in prison.

I do have a problem with men that call themselves, "Straight", "A Real Nigga", a "G", or "Thorough", but you're creeping on the down-low fucking another man in his butt or getting sum head from a homosexual. Doing any of those things makes you a homosexual too, so don't lie to yourself. Just be honest and keep it real with yourself. It's a lot of dudes like that who get out of prison and hit the streets linking up with sister's/women and giving the female all kinds of STD's. That's that shit I don't agree with. What's done in the dark, my guy, will come to the light. So, don't think you're slicker than a can of oil because you're not.

Here's one more extra one I have to add to this brief list of do's and don'ts in prison. Rule 6: Debt. Do not borrow something from a fellow man or run up a high bill getting things from a fellow prisoner not knowing whether or not you will be able to pay that person back. I've seen many conflicts occur because of debt. With that being said, your only goal in prison should be transforming yourself into a better person and learning exactly what you must do in order to survive. Understand who your real enemies are in this environment. They are the judiciary/courts, police, your attorney, the district attorney prosecutor, judge, parole board, and probation officer. These are your enemies.

Don't scheme on another prisoner unless they had a part in you ending up here. If they did then that's strictly between you and them. But don't take your personal problems or frustrations out on the next person that had nothing to do with your confinement. You have to elevate your mind to the next level of thinking so that you may better deal with the harsh reality of being incarcerated. Now, what I had to do to prepare my mental mindset for was choose a strategy to counter what the prison system was designed to do to me.

I knew before I went into the Federal Prison System that I had to make some serious adjustments and get serious about my life. I had to awaken myself from the false dreams and fantasies of living the type of illusional lifestyle I had been leading all of my life. It was these fantasies and misguided goals that led me to this point in the first place. Prison is no joke unless you're a fool or a clown. Prison is designed to break your spirits and to destroy your resolve. They want you to become a lesser man when it's all said and done.

The administration and prison authorities will try to exploit your weaknesses, destroy your initiative, and negate all signs of individuality. I stood strong to their evil power and didn't play any games with them. I never laughed or joked because there was nothing fun nor funny about my situation. I advise anyone not to come to prison and waste time playing around. Shit is real in here. If you're in prison, use your time wisely. Go into the law-library and fight your case. That's one of the smartest and most valuable ways to do time. You have to do the time; you can't allow the time to do you. This was my mentality every day because I knew what I was up against.

My survival depended on understanding what the prison authority were always plotting to do to me. I was a rebellious, conscious, and revolutionary individual who bucked against the system. I did my best to share my understanding, my experience, wisdom, and knowledge with the inexperienced younger prisoners and other men on how this system is set up to work against us. Most of the time my advice fell on deaf ears, but I was ok with that. I understood that a man was going to do what he wanted to do and that everyone came around on their own time.

In 1992, I was in the Tennessee State Prison System. At that time, I was in the prime years of my life. I had a pretty good street rep and was a wild hothead. I was highly feared, respected, and well connected throughout the T.D.O.C. I was at this particular prison called The Turney Center, amongst a lot of my homeboys from Nashville, Tennessee, which we redubbed Cashville, Ten-A-Key. I saw an opportunity to form a unit amongst us. We all stuck together as a clique, but the jail administration looked at us as a gang.

I never saw myself joining a street gang such as the Crip & Bloods, the G.D's, and Vice Lords. At the time in my generation and era growing up in South Nashville, there wasn't any gangs in my neighborhood. A homie that I am no longer friends with came up with the name "Royal Gangsters", however I was the one to put-it-down, formulate it, and bring the real thorough brothers together. The rest of my guys liked my idea and we joined forces and became a force to be reckoned with. We had a very good rapport with another organization from out of West, Tennessee who was known as "The Memphis Mob." Shout out to my guy "Eddie Red Depriest" and R.I.P. "King Fish", and George Monroe. These were the two founders of the M-Mob.

I had become the founder and leader of the notorious Royal Gangsters. My comrades and I were all from Cashville. The only way you could become a member was if you were from there as well. The purpose of our movement and structure was designed primarily to strive in a positive and economical direction towards growth, change, development, and transforming our minds by rehabilitating ourselves while in prison. We stood up against any other transgression towards our beliefs, values, principles, and what we stood for.

We fought against tyranny, discrimination, and oppression from the administration. We also would defend ourselves against any outside group, clique, gang, or organization etc. We never started anything with anyone else, but we would always handle our wax. We were about our business, and we didn't duck no rec. (point, blank, period...) When Black men unite together in any type of way, functioning on a fundamental form of unity, the white authorities/administration get scared and terrified. The truth of the matter is that they are the real "GANG" and the only gang on the yard with real power.

The threat of seeing Black men at peace and unified makes them paranoid because they fear that we will then rise against them. They don't want to see Black men come together for a common cause under one umbrella. This is why the enemy uses all different types of tactics against us to keep us at odds with each other. They are experts of the classic war strategy of divide and conquer. They used that back in slavery on the plantation. That divide and conquer method has been used for over 400 years now. What's even sadder is that they've refined that strategy year after year to the point where it runs on autopilot within our community.

We the Royal Gangsters stood together, supported each other, and gained strength from each other. Although we didn't have strength in numbers, we were all-natural born warriors, fighters, street soldiers who had big balls and heart. Each man could stand alone on his own two feet. Whatever we had we shared and multiplied it and made it grow. Whatever we learned, we shared with our fellow brothers. This act of sharing and empowering each other multiplied our strength tenfold. That is not to say that we were all alike in our own responses to hardships that we suffered.

All men have different breaking points and react differently to stress. However, it is the responsibility of the stronger ones to raise up the weaker ones so that we all become stronger in the process. As a leader, one must sometimes take actions that are unpopular or will produce results that won't be seen until years down the line. You must also know how to make quick decisions that will be in the best interest of all your comrades. Most importantly, you must have knowledge or experience that you can share with your people to empower them and help them

Being qualified to lead it takes many qualities within oneself. Honesty and patience are two very important components. Self-control is also paramount for you can't lead off of emotion. People are entrusting you with their lives as a leader, so you must be rational at all times. Also, never send someone to a place you wouldn't go yourself, and never give an order you wouldn't carry out yourself. The struggle that we fought (and continue to fight in prison) is just a microcosm of the struggle as a whole. The racism and repression on the inside are just the same as it is on the outside.

Prison and the administration authorities conspire to rob each man of his dignity. I made a vow not to let that happen to me. I would survive any man or institution that tries to rob me of my dignity, my manhood, my honor, my principles, and integrity. I will not part with it no matter what, regardless of the circumstances of pressure. I'm a strong Asiatic, Black man. Like my father before me, I had been groomed to be an intellect and a wise man. Although, I had chosen to take a different path and lifestyle, I tried in my own fashion to live up to the principles and responsibilities of the role my father left for me.

Prison is a still point in a turning world, and it is very easy to remain stuck in the same place while the rest of the world moves on. It's all about educating your mind to a higher degree; seek knowledge, wisdom, understanding, and most of all, truth. I believe 100% that I have evolved. I've been self-evaluating and educating non-stop. I do a lot self-studying on my current condition and stay on top of my health. I check my mental every day, control my emotions and anger, and keep my ego in check for destiny rules us all.

There is no sense in being afraid of what lies ahead waiting around the corner. Whether it is good or evil, it will be there waiting patiently. Discovery is what comes at the end of each voyage. Sometimes the voyage is planned out and attacked like a quest brought forth through intuition. Other times a man is swept along carelessly at the mercy of whatever life reveals to him. The discoveries all ultimately add up to one thing. That one thing is true knowledge of self. The voyage may be rough just as much as it is enjoyable. But in the end, you must have the strength to accept the truth once it is revealed to you.

Drive, not talent, is what separates the 10% of the world from the rest of the other 90%. Everyone has enough talent to achieve a level of excellence that would bring them the perfect amount of sustenance. The telling fact is that some just don't have enough of a hunger to use that talent to make something extraordinary happen. Understanding that $1,000,000 is a dream for one man, comfortable for another, and broke to the next man, is key to taking the action necessary to bring dreams to fruition. Being comfortable in any position leads to complacency, and most people would rather be complacent than hungry.

Make the simple decision to satisfy your hunger and pursue a dream so relentlessly that you become a part of the 10%.

CHAPTER 36

Prison Re-entry and The Sentencing Project

Nashville, Tennessee: Dee 50 years old, Monster 55, and Don-Don 26, all have one thing in common. All three have felony arrest on their records and all three have served time in the Tennessee State Prison System. These three men each gave me a snapshot of what their daily life is like.

Dee: "Man, these folks out here are something else with their hateful selves. Ain't no decent jobs out here for brothers like me. All people are talking about is be patient, but I have a family to feed—three daughters and four sons. It's difficult when you have this big 'X' or strike on your back that's called a felony. It puts you in restricted category box; a misfit type of group that society has outcasts as being unworthy being considered a regular citizen. Because of these limitations, a lot of brothers hit the concrete running to the block and picking up that sack to get that money. It's a cold dog ass world out here. It takes capital, dividends, or some type of income to survive.

The cost of living in Cashville is high as hell compared to 20 years ago..."

Monster: "Man I have two murders on my criminal record, one attempted murder, and three drug cases under my resume. I am an arm-career criminal on paper for 8 years of parole. I ain't trying to go back to prison. I'd rather die and go to jail than have to come back here and smell another man's shit, farts, arms, feet, and ass. Three hots and a hard ass bunk. That's why I got me two jobs right now. I say this here, if you're work inside prison for 28 cents an hour, why not work in the free world making at least $10 an hour? You might not be making what you want, but at least you have a better opportunity to control your destiny. You just have to be willing to work. You have to have some type of motivation and drive. Some people do, and some don't..."

Don-Don: "I am facing parole violations if I don't find employment by next month. It's a part of my parole stipulations and just don't know if I'm going to be able to do it (find a job). I have no work skills, no G.E.D. or high school diploma. All I know is selling drugs and hustling in the streets..." These are the struggles of a few brothers trying to adjust to life on the outside. Now look at this, just to show you how the corruption unfolds and the people in higher up positions works and scheme a Washington-based sentencing project and New York-based Vera Institute of Justice both support a Jan 27, 2012 report from the six year federally funded Justice Reinvestment Initiative.

This initiative was designed to identify and implement "cost efficient, evidence-based criminal justice reforms using methods from 17 states that are supposed to save taxpayers $3.3 billion over the next 10 years". Promises are fine but the money isn't getting to communities of color who are disproportionately affected by the large numbers of people in state and local jails. A minister in Milwaukee Pastors of the United Methodists of Milwaukee complained that grassroots activists in Milwaukee were not getting the resources or information.

He is quoted as saying, "re-entry is huge here in Milwaukee. Most of the Black male population has had some type of contact with prison. The young men congregate in our neighborhoods, drinking and selling drugs, seemingly unable to find work. Their unemployment rate is nearly 60%. I am getting calls daily about this. We need to mobilize everyone and direct their attention to how to solve this problem". he said.

Pastors of the United Methodists in Milwaukee is a church coalition that was founded to focus attention on issues important to the Black Community. Some of the churches provided limited direct service to former inmates. There is no clear discussion about what money is available to pay for re-entry programs.

Minister L. said, "the big Think Tanks are getting funds, but the money isn't coming down to the people dealing with the program".

The sentencing project issue a report in Jan 24, 2014 saying one in three states closed prisons between 2011 and 2013, which saved an estimated $1.2 Billion. The Urban Institute also released a report in Jan.27 predicting that at the current pace $4.6 Billion could be saved in coming years as state prisons populations are reduced. Some analysts noted federal support for Justice Investment Initiative has been a meager $6 Million annually, but before President Obama left office, he convinced Congress to appropriate $28 million for that fiscal year it was debated upon.

CHAPTER 37

Women Prison and Sexual Assault

Correctional officers all across the United States are responsible for most of prison's sexual assaults. A new Justice Department study shows that allegations of sex abuse in the nation's prisons and jails are increasing—with correctional officers responsible for half of it. However, prosecution for this type of sexual misconduct is still extremely rare. The report released by the Bureau of Justice Statistics takes data collected by correctional administrators who represent all of the nation's federal and state prisons. as well as many county jails.

This report shows that administrators logged more than 8,000 reports of abuse to their overseers each year between 2009 and 2011. This is up 11% from the department's previous report that was covering 2007 and 2008. It's not clear whether the increase is the result of better reporting or does represent an actual rise in the number of incidents. The Justice

Department Statistician who authored the report told Pro Public that abuse allegations might be increasing because of growing awareness of the 2003 Prison Rape elimination act.

"It's a matter of speculation, but certainly there's been a considerable effort to inform staff about the dangers for sexual misconduct, so we could be seeing the impact of that of that", said the Justice Department Statistician.

The report also showed a growing proportion of the allegations have been dismissed by prison officials as "unfounded" or "unsubstantiated" after investigation. But even in the rare cases where there is enough evidence to prove that sexual abuse has occurred, and that a correctional officer is responsible for it, the perpetrator rarely faces prosecution. While prison staff shown to be involved in sexual misconduct lose their jobs, fewer than half are referred for prosecution, and only 1% ultimately got convicted.

One third of staff caught abusing prisoners are allowed to resign before an investigation ensues the report concluded. This means that there's no public record of what exactly transpired and nothing preventing a prison official from getting a similar job at another prison or jail facility. "These findings point to a level of impunity in our prisons and jails across America that is simply unacceptable", said the Executive Director of Justice Detention International, which is a prison advocacy group in California.

"When correctional agents don't punish or choose to ignore sexual abuse and rape committed by staff members-- people who are paid by our tax dollars to keep inmates safe--they support criminal behavior".

The lack of punishment may deter inmates from reporting. When the Justice Department has surveyed inmates directly, as opposed to the administrators that oversee them, the report of abuse has been for greater. A 2013 survey estimated that out of the 2.2 million men, women, and children locked up in America's human warehouses, more than 80,000 prisoners have been sexually victimized by fellow inmates and staff over a two-year period— roughly five times the rate reported by administrators.

"Inmates don't report because of the way the institutions handle these complaints. They're afraid if they report, then the staff will retaliate", said a law professor at the University of Southern California who studies the issue. "Even if you report and they believe you, which they probably won't, the most likely thing to happen is that the person will be suspended or may be fired..."

CHAPTER 38

Exoneration

In 2013, a record-breaking new report on "Exonerations" for innocent people convicted of crimes in the United States was released by the Registry of Exonerations. The new report found that 87 exonerations were recorded in 2013 were more than in any of the past 25 years. About one-third of those 87 were in cases where no crime was committed. The registry had been in the works for a few years as a joint project of the University of Michigan Law School and the Center on Wrongful Convictions at Northwestern University school of law.

Its lists information on cases from 1989 through 2014 in which people were wrongly convicted of crimes and later cleared of all charges based on new evidence. "The registry crimes went public in May 2012 and the more researchers looked, the more they found," said by the Senior Researcher for the registry. "There's 1,300 cases and exponentially every one of those is a story of tragedy, not just for the wrongfully convicted but for family members and for other victims who find out later that the real perpetrator has gone on to commit other crimes."

The report indicates that contrary to popular belief, the number of exonerations involving DNA has gradually declined since 2005, and only represented about a fifth of the total number of exonerations in 2013. In the same period, the number of non-exonerations per year doubled from 34 in 2005 to 69 in 2013 the report read. 15 of the 87 known exonerations in 2013 occurred in cases where defendants were convicted after pleading guilty. Most exonerations studied each year were homicide and sexual assault cases.

There were 40 Murder exonerations in 2013, including one involving a prisoner who'd been sentenced to death, and 18 that involved rape or other sexual assaults. The Research Senior explained the victims came forward and admitted that they had lied in those cases, and in others as well murder was proven to be accidents. A Chicago Mother was convicted in 2005 of murdering her four-year old son. She served 7 years of a 30-year sentence before being released. The mother was exonerated in 2013 after evidence revealed police coerced her into confessing, and that her son's brother saw him wrap an elastic band around his neck while he was playing "Spiderman", according to the registry.

The report has listed the following 10 states with

the most recorded exonerations in 2013: #1).Texas-13, #2).Illinois-9, #3).New York-8, #4)Washington-7, #5)California-6, #6)Michigan-5, #7)Missouri-5, #8) Connecticut-4, #9)Georgia-4 and #10) Virginia-4. The states with most recorded exonerations are not necessarily those where most false convictions have occurred, researchers noted. 33 known exonerations in 2013 were obtained with law enforcement cooperation. According to researchers, police and prosecutors appear to be taking increasingly active roles in reinvestigating possible false convictions, and to be more responsive to claims of innocence from convicted defendants.

Senior Researcher said it's encouraging to law enforcement—including prosecutors and police—be a bit more proactive and willing to have an open mind that wrongful convictions can happen. "Finding the truth should be the common goal, but there's still some resistance", he said.

"When defense lawyers, innocence projects, or even defendants alert prosecutors to mistakes, historically the response has been the jury and courts have spoken", Mr. Possley said. "Some Prosecutors fight against motions to have DNA testing done, but why?" Mr. Possley asked. "It's coming from this historical position of we got it right. Don't question our Authority", Senior Researcher explained. "The ability to DNA test for more than two decades has provided clear lessons and sent a clear message", he continued. "Witnesses lie. Police lie. Defense lawyers don't do their jobs. Prosecutors hide evidence. Forensics testing makes mistakes, or they intentionally mislead. These things happen".

He added, "They have to get past the feeling that making a mistake is a sign of weakness...nobody wants to convict an innocent person, but who wants to admit that they did? That's hard!"

CHAPTER 39

Federal and State Geographical Division

What is Time and Geographical Division defined by Prison terms? Time is the duration or length of one's incarceration. Geographic Division is the geographic standards that separates prisoners from one another, whether it's by cities, states, and different countries. The division can be also based on non-geographical characteristics such as race, culture, or religion. Here I have four prisoners who will tell you their story and their experience pertaining to division within prison. The first prisoner we will here from is Brother-X. Currently, Brother-X is serving a life sentence.

***

Brother-X

What's good ya'll. I'm Brother-X and I'm currently service a life sentence. How do I feel about it? Man, it's fucked up, excuse my French. I ain't gonna lie, I'm a bitter nigga after being railroaded and lynched in those devil's courtroom. I try to stay spiritual, grounded, humble, and allow "Allah" to seek justice for me. My own way of handling things seems to always get me into more trouble. Sure enough, thanks to "Allah" and our President Barack Obama the Arm Career Criminal Act 924-C will reduce my sentence.

For the most part, I remain optimistic about my day-to-day life. I rely on my Islamic faith and hope for the best outcome on my appeal. So, with that being said, I just take it one day at a time. I'm remain laid back, chilling, maintaining, and staying focused while the show goes on inside of this mad house called prison. What are the types of things that go in prison? Man, you don't want to know. In my opinion, it be all types of negative, ignorant bullshit going on in here. And it's always over petty shit too.

A lot of prison politicking goes on in these United States Penitentiary yards. It's very geographical. Everyone splits themselves off into groups that go by various names: "Cars", "Gangs", "Organizations", etc... The division is also based on race too. You have Blacks, Hispanics, Whites, Native Indians, Pacific Islander's / Asian's, all five shades in the human race in here who keep to themselves. A car defines where you're from and who you're riding with; whether it's a certain state, race, or gang affiliation.

Me, I'm from Houston, Texas. Before I became Nation-of-Islam, I rocked with Texas all day. Texas is the South, so wherever you are from, or what you claiming that's more likely what you are standing for...ya' understand? You have the East Coast which is up top, then the West Coast and the Midwest. The South consists of all the states in the bottom of the map: Texas, Louisiana, Tennessee, Alabama, Georgia, Arkansas, Florida, North Carolina, South Carolina, and Mississippi.

Everyone be trippin' about where there'll from, but I be on some other type of shit. As far as being Black, Black men we're all in the same conditions and predicament. We are warehoused in this modern-day slavery here on the new plantation—prison. As a Black man, I feel that us collectively as Black men be stuck on some ignorant, foul, and stupid shit. They got that willie lynch syndrome and crabs-in-the-bucket mentality real bad. There's so much self-hatred built up that it makes it easy to divide and conquer us. Here's a good example.

A new brother arrives to prison fresh off the bus and walks into the housing block in a housing unit. The first thing the other brothers will ask the new arrival is, "Say, brother where is you from?" The new brother might say, "I'm from New York". The group of brothers will then say, "Oh, your homies over there at the chess table". The energy behind that whole exchange is, "Fuck buddy...he ain't from where I'm from!" This is the type of mentality we as Black Men have to deal with daily inside the belly of this beast.

We don't treat or embrace each other (Black Men) with love and respect like we should. I'm not saying *that all Black men act in this form of fashion because there are some very intelligent, conscious, good, and humble brothers in here in the prison system. I'm just saying this after observing the flip side of this equation. A Mexican or White person can come through the door off the bus and their people show love off the rip. No matter what city or state he's from, they are going to make sure he gets all the necessities he needs: care package, shoes, hygiene kit, etc.*

A Black Man catch pure hell from both the prison staff/administration and then from his own counterparts. It's a geographical epidemic going on throughout the entire F.B.O.P. It's a mad house inside these USP's. We are the only race of people with no unity amongst us. So, I stay in my own lane and I keep my circle small. I only have a few associates. That's the only way to rock. It's so much division amongst us Black Men in this prison environment. Man, we some lost brother's up in this system. There are men who are aware of the plight against us designed by our true enemies, but the majority of us are sleep. We got a lot of work to do Black Men. We got to tighten up and get some order in our lives...!

***

<u>Brother 'P'</u>

What's up... This "P. I am serving 15 years for Meth. I've been down on my bid for 12 years now. I'm down with the independent white boys from Mississippi. I grew up around Black people, so I run with the Blacks too. No disrespect to my Caucasian Race, but I'm not racist. I view this Geographical situation for what it is. In this USP, it's very segregated when it comes to other races integrating or kicking-it together. In here, and on any USP yard, you just can't rotate how you want to with other races.

My people be on that Racist-White Supremacy shit real tough. Me, I'm not with that racist shit. My wife is Spanish, and my best friend Mike is Black. I've caught some real serious static a couple times from my white counterparts because of how I get down. The Aryan Brotherhood, The Aryan Circle, and the Skinheads didn't like how I rotated and associated with Blacks. They basically they tried to dictate how I do my time, which resulted in me being stabbed up on three different occasions.

I survived each attack by the grace of God. After the last attempt on my life, I ended up catching a body. I had no choice but to defend myself—they were trying to take my life. Thankfully, the murder charge was dropped against me. After standing my ground for ten calendar years, not ducking no reck, I finally got the respect I deserved. I don't mess with nobody unless they bring drama to me. I stay in my lane and do me. But there are a lot of hateful, angry, psycho, and miserable men running around bitter because they are here in prison. Misery loves company.

I thank God that I am at the end of my sentence now. I have learned a lot by being in prison, especially in these USP Prisons. I'm going to try everything in my power not to come back to prison once I get out. I got three kids out in the free world that's depending on me to come home too. This crazy geographical division is the way of life behind these USP walls. Those are the prison rules, I didn't set the convict rules. I just had to learn the hard way how to adapt, adjust, and survive by them, the very same rules that almost stole my life from me. So, beware of what's going on, and most importantly, be careful who you choose to run with in Prison...

***

<u>Brother-T</u>

My name is "T". I'm from Chattooga, TN. I'm riding under the six-point-star, 74 (G.D.) Gangster Disciple. That's how I'm rocking. About this Geographical Division cycle here on these USP Yards it ain't no joke. I run with my "Folks", reppin' those pitchforks...My give or take, It's a thing like this here. Here's a scenario. I'm from Chatt-town, but I'm on count with my team, so it goes without saying what it is with me. Here's a prime example of how ugly shit can be and go from 0-to-100 in the blink of an eye.

Say for instance, if the Tennessee car and my folks

bump heads and clash. It ain't no secret or mystery who I'm siding with. When the shit hit the fan, I have to get at the Tennessee car by all means necessary. War is War. Because with me, I am who I am. I can't fake the funk. It ain't no faking with me. I been G.D. since I was 14-years old. I'm 32 now. I'mma die with my head held up high, to the clear blue sky, it's 74 till the world blow. I hate that it has to be this way. But it is what it is. Unfortunately, this is way the way the state and federal system is set up to be.

It's by design that the prison administration wants to keep every group, organization, or other race of people hating and going against each other because of the fear of us going against them. That's how I see it. An incident occurred when I was at USP Pollock in Louisiana. The administration pitted us G.D.s against The D.C. car and a lot of good men got hurt real bad. Yeah, this thing on the geographical division is propaganda at its rawest forms.

The prison officials from the top all the way down know about tensions between different groups of prisoners and create the circumstances for war to occur. The Mexicans against other Mexicans, Blacks against whites, or whoever it might go down with. The D.C. Blacks they stay in conflict with everybody. They are so confrontational because they are large in number. When you get 300 to 400 of them on one yard, they be with the shit.

One thing I can say about them is that they stick

together no matter what. Although we bump heads with them a lot throughout the F.B.O.P., they go hard and are about that work. They ain't ducking no rec at all. When you get into an altercation with them you better be ready to work, because they are coming at your ass with those knives. When we got into it with them, I was stabbed in the head four times, in the shoulders, and hit once in the side. My left lung collapsed. I had to be airlifted to the outside hospital, I almost lost my life. It was all over a game of basketball.

You gotta be prepared to push on your line and be trained to go whenever your team encounters a situation...

***

Brother-B

I go by "B" and I'm from New Orleans, Louisiana. What up whoadie? I'm here all day, I got a life sentence up in this bitch. I only fuck with my rounds; we from Uptown N.O. That's where Baby and Slim of Ca$h Money Records is from. Yeah that's my round and he holding it down fo' tha' Uptown.

Anyway, during my 17 years in a U.S.P. I've seen a lot. When I came inside, I got straight on my grind. I met a lot of good men, and unfortunately, I've also been in the presence of some real snakes. I'm probably one of the few that actually likes how this prison setting is designed to be. Prison life isn't made to be easy or pleasant. Too many people get too comfortable in here and lose touch with reality. You have to be a cold, fearless, dominant to survive in here. It's simply predator vs. prey all day in prison.

Round, I've seen firsthand how crazy shit can get in here. The division amongst us that fuels the violence is crazy. Within Louisiana, we have New Orleans, Baton Rouge, Lake Charles, Shreveport, and all the other cities bumping head inside the Louisiana car. One city always thinks that their city is better or harder than the next city. What's crazy is how quickly we're ready to go to war all over this dumb, superficial shit.

No disrespect to the citizens of New Orleans because my heritage, family, and my life is there but fuck those racist ass crackas who gave me my life sentence. Why should I care for that city and be ready to go to war inside of this prison car over a city or state that fucking buried me alive—you heard me. Those crackas don't have no love nor respect for Black lives. You see how they broke the levees and put our city under water during Hurricane Katrina. I knew a lot of people and families who lost everything they ever had when that happened: houses, property, valuable possessions, and family members.

Currently, my case is on appeal right now. I'm looking good in court now. Witnesses have recanted their story; police were found to have selected a biased crime scene for evidence, and the prosecutor was found to have hidden evidence in court and choosing a biased jury. I can see a brighter day after this is over, I am shining like a diamond. My lawyer assured me that I am getting some get back on my appeal when the case is overturned. I can't wear this life sentence anymore because I have outgrown —you heard me.

By the time I get re-sentenced, I'll get a reduction down to 20 years, which will kick me straight out the front door. I plan to get back to that money once I get out. I got kids at home to put through college. It won't be long now. For now, I'm just keeping myself out of the way in this bitch. If some funk jump off, it's enough rounds that can handle it and take care of the problem. Not me, I'm not jeopardizing my freedom for the bullshit. I'm patiently waiting for my blessing to come.

My advice to anyone locked down behind these walls' is don't get caught up in the nonsense. If you are going to fight, fight the good cause. Fight your case in that law library and give that time back to those devil's. I'm out whoadie!

CHAPTER 40

Misdirection

Misdirection is the teaching style of the devil and here's the curriculum. Captivate 50 million viewers worldwide with reality T.V each night, but never show families destroyed by drugs, AIDS, and mass incarceration. Paint a picture that makes everyone stop and stare. Show them a picture of the ultra-rich, ultra-beautiful, and super powerful. Make everyone concentrate on that picture and wonder how they can become a part of it. Blind them with the glare of an easy life filled with sunshine, sex, and self-indulgence. Wait until they forget everything else that matters like family, friends, children, and God.

If they start to snap out of the hypnotic state, sedate them with music, movies, and filthy books filled with none-sense. As they pour out the desires of their hearts, entice them with all things that they fancy. Treat every vice with an addiction. Numb the minds with small crimes against humanity, until atrocities are accepted as everyday occurrences. Let all things that are detestable to the creator become the things that are bragged about until good becomes bad, and bad becomes good.

We have to redirect our energy and thoughts in the way we think. We've been misdirected for much too long...

CHAPTER 41

The Company You keep

It is better to be alone than to be in the wrong company. Tell me who your best friends are, and I can tell you who you are. They say that "Birds of a feather flock together", and "if you lie down with dogs, you wake up with fleas". If you run with wolves, you will learn how to howl. And if you associate with eagles, you will learn how to soar high to great heights. A mirror reflects a man's face, but what he is really like is shown by the kind of friends he chooses.

The simple, but true fact of life is that you become like those with whom you closely associate for good and bad. The less you associate with some people, the more your life will improve. Any time you tolerate mediocrity in others, you tolerate more of it in yourself. An important attribute in successful people is their impatience with negative thinking and negative acting people. As you grow, your associates change. Some of your friends will not want you to go on. They will want you to stay where they are. Friends that don't help you climb will want you to crawl. Your friends will either grow your vision or choke your dreams. Those that don't increase you will eventually decrease you and your values.

Consider this:
We never receive counsel from unproductive people. Never discuss your problems with someone incapable of contributing to the solution, because those who never succeeded themselves are always the first to tell you how. Not everyone has a right to speak about your life. You are certain to get the worst of the bargain when you exchange ideas with the wrong person.

Don't follow anyone who's not going anywhere. With some people you spend an evening: with others you invest it. Be careful where you stop to inquire for directions along the road of life. Wise is the person who fortifies his life with the right friendships...

CHAPTER 42

Seeds of Destruction

Seeds of destruction are negative words, images, and concepts that enter the mind and take hold within them. Thoughts that are produced by seeds of destruction develop a false perception. How we perceive a thing or circumstance determines how we deal with it because our perception drives our reality. Seeds of destruction can make a strong man weak, and a weak man kill. Seeds of destruction distort reality. Once your reality becomes distorted you lose your sense of reason and you make bad choices.

You see how the young white supremacist man in South Carolina in 2015 killed those nine Black people in the Church and how the other man in Nashville, Tennessee shot and killed the young people at the Waffle House. These are just a few prominent incidents we can think of. You see those gentleman's reality was distorted, which lead them to bad choices. Those bad choices turn into bad deeds, and bad deeds are the next seeds of destruction into another weak mind.

The weak mind is symbolic of being bitten by a poisonous snake. If you're not immune to the venom, or don't have the cure, you will die. In other words: people who plant seeds of destruction are snakes. If you're not conscious or aware that a snake is planting seeds in your mind you will allow those seeds to grow to the point when you become a tool of the snake. I see many men in the prison system day-by-day swallow the poisonous seeds of destruction.

If you are a tool being used by a snake, you're dead. However, if you're immune, the seeds of destruction planted by the snake die before they grow anymore. The cure to poisonous seeds of destruction is consciousness. To understand consciousness, you must know what unconsciousness is.

Unconsciousness is being naive. Consciousness is being aware and hip to what's happening in and around you at all times. When the snake knows that you're up on his or her scheme they understand that biting you is suicide.

However, that doesn't stop the snake from looking for fertile soil in which to plant his seeds of destruction. So, I tell you now to do one thing: think! Use your head, cut your grass, so you can see those poisonous snakes and get them from around you...

CHAPTER 43

Dealing With the Loss of A loved One

Men and Women who are locked up go through many trials and tribulations in prison. When things seem to be getting better, often there is another hardship that's waiting around the corner. The worst thing that can happen to a prisoner is losing a loved one, especially a child or parent. We can't even attend their funerals to pay our respect. The prison authorities rejoice in seeing the hurt and pain inside of prisoners who go through such grief.

How do we deal with the loss of a loved one under these circumstances? There are no easy answers. I have lost almost my entire family while I've been incarcerated for the past 26 calendar years. I've lost my Mother, my Father, three Uncles, two Aunts, six Cousins, one Niece, three of my Nephews, my Grandmother and Grandfather. I was devasted with each passing death. I was crashed beyond any hurt could fathom. It is natural to grieve over the physical loss of a loved one. But when you lose so many at once you become numb to it. Whenever I receive bad news from home it feels normal in a way, because everyone I ever loved has passed on.

I have come to understand and realize that every human being that was born into this world was born to die. We can cheat our way through life, but we can't escape death. From dust we were created, to dust we shall return. Life is full of splendor and beauty once you discover what your purpose is and why you were put on this earth. You must search for that purpose while you journey through life and fulfill every single essence in which God created you in to be perfect reflection of Him. Some will never be, but God gave every human being a special gift and sometimes it takes a person a lifetime to figure it out, God's plan.

But dealing with the loss of my loved ones, I just shut down and don't want to be bothered with anyone. I try to hold the hurt and pain inside, and not deal with other people. To some who don't know me very well they might think I was just a miserable and bitter person. However, the people that truly know understand what I'm going through. I'm thankful for them and their help with me coping with the situation.

Dearest love ones who have passed on, you all are still a part of me. Spiritually, we still have that connection that will never decease. In me they live, and through me they will continue to live just as the many other men and women whose incarcerated family members will continue to live through them. As long as you're alive, your family can never die. As the author of this great, significant book I encourage every human being whose locked up to utilize your time wisely. Find your purpose in life and strive for change.

Prison is a mind-state. You are the product of your thoughts. As a man thinks, so is he. Don't allow your past to dictate your future. We all make mistakes, we're all human. If you have suffered the loss of a loved one, I pray it strengthens you and that you find solace in others who may have experienced the same pain. A kind word of condolence is like a good dose of medicine, gratitude heals the broken hearted. Peace, stay positive, stay force!

CHAPTER 44/44A

Work

Work what is work? By dictionary terms work is defined as, "labor; employment; task; a place where industrial labor is done". It can also mean, "forces × distance, the exertion of energy on an object". No matter how much force applied, if the result is not motion then no work has been done. To create and to build something of great value you have to endure the process and put in the work.

Work is a strenuous activity that involves difficulty and extreme effort, and usually affords no immediate pleasure. To carry out work it requires strength, effort, will, and most importantly, sacrifice and disciple. One of the best sources of joy in this world is the feeling you get when you have honestly succeeded in accomplishing a righteous, self-deserved goal. The sense of achievement is a wonderful bliss.

What are you working towards in your daily life? I'm sure that every human being alive is working towards some type of goal, whether they are consciously aware of it or not. They are in tune and in harmony with gravity. Work must be done no matter how we define or see it. It cannot be excluded from the source of life. We have to work steady in a fast-moving world that's constantly changing to make the most of ourselves...

CHAPTER 45/44B

Two Paths: One decision

As I currently serve a lengthy federal prison sentence, I often look around at my surroundings and environment and wonder how many men I will see who will find themselves back in this situation after being released. The reason being is the vast majority of the prison population can't seem to break away from the recreation, "sport and play". It's the *I'm just killing time* way of thinking. On any given day inside of the belly of this beast one can see the video watchers geeking, reality show kings, the chess players, the card champions, the weight pile junkies, or professional prison sports participants. There's an understanding that most of these activities are used as stress relievers or for recreational purposes. We should use them as such.

True indeed most of us feel like we've been punished too severely and that may be the case. However, what you do while in prison as men and women will determine your worth and need in society. It goes without saying that we owe it to ourselves as individuals to lead better lives. But let's look at this from a different perspective. We as prisoners have family and friends alike who believe in and support us. They send their hard-earned money, books, cards, letters, and other tokens of love to let us know that we are not alone.

Now the question is, how do we expect our families to respond to us wasting years in prison, not even making an attempt to do better? This is disrespectful to us, as well as our loved ones. No disrespect intended to lifers or the people on Death Row, but please allow me to use your situation as an eye opener. For those of us who are going home to family soon let us look at the drive of those that have no out dates. If they can plan and try to create a future where there is little-to-no hope for one, then what's wrong with us?

Never allow anyone nor anything to kill your dreams. You as an individual must respect them enough to pursue them without fail. Yes, we have the right to make our own decisions. However, we are not privileged to choose the perfect outcome of our choices. Think of all the tears that have been shed regarding your predicament whether they were yours or someone else's. Think of all the times you wished you had done things differently. Allow these thoughts to be the fuel to motivate you along your path. If that's not enough then read this last statement from one who is no longer among the living anymore. These are a man's last words from Death Row two minutes before his execution.

February 2, 1994 Offender Last Statement:

"I wish that I could take away all that I've done and be given the chance to do things concealed in my dreams, like watching my children grow up into adults, taking trips with my family, or seeing the proud look on my mother's face at the outcome of my life. However, this day will never come for me. My life must end because of a foolish mistake. I just want all to know that this is not the way to die. Sometimes we don't learn our life's lesson until it's too late and other times our "sorries" are not enough. God please forgive me of all my sins, look after my family and protect them. Please let the family of the deceased know in their hearts that I'm sorry for ending the life of their loved one. Lord, I am ready, take me home with you. Amen...

Final Thoughts:

Accept conditions as they exist and accept responsibility for changing them. "When we least expect it, life sets us a challenge. At such a moment, there is no point in pretending that nothing has happened or in saying that we are not ready.

The Challenge will not wait. Life does not look back. A week is more than enough time for us to decide whether or not to accept our destiny" ...

CHAPTER 46/45B

Prison Poems

"Pen and paper…"

*Pen was quite a handsome guy
that had a magnificent way with words,
And paper was a pretty attractive girl
Both living in a small caged world…
Pen met paper one day
While the sun was shining bright up in the
Sky
Paper blush as her infatuation
grew into a crush
Pen felt the chemistry and gave paper
A noticeable wink…
And
Out of pen's love for paper
they develop ink…
And as ink grew
Pen and paper… Gave birth to
Words…
Pen loves her girl paper… So together they
Wrote the magical book on love…!*

"In Prison..."

In Prison, you don't have to be in prison,
while you're lockup,
Keep your mind open and think clever like a fox,
Don't allow your brain to not think outside the box.
Time never stands still, it waits for no one,
One day you here, the next day, you gone.
Every man or woman wish in prison,
Is too one day make it home.
Time in prison can change a person in so many ways,
Time can turn youth into old age.
In Prison, men stay angry, and full of rage, by treated
Like animals' lockup in a cage.
In Prison, every criminal has one thing for sure in
common, everyone here is identified by a number.
In Prison, I've been known to be violent, vicious, and
ruthless, and don't need number's
Because Prison and life lessons has taught me to be humble.
In Prison, some men call cells their home,
It's just a little place, with a little space,
Like a lion in a cage, he has no room to roam
In Prison, some men out date ain't nowhere near,
It's just too many Blacks in prison, that shouldn't be here.
In prison, It's geographical, territorial, and racist,
All type of politicking goes on,
I've seen a man get killed for disrespecting another man,
While he was on the phone.
In Prison, It's C.O.'s versus convicts,
Everyone hates a cop
It's a lot of Black on Black crime,

When is it going to stop?
It's White Pride if you Aryan Nation,
It's Muslim if you submit to "Allah" creation,
It's prohibited to eat pork and bacon", Greeting's,
As Salaam Alaikum.
It's a lot of brother's wit dreads, but they ain't Rasta.
It's the Italians that love to eat pasta
And most of them somehow connected to the mafia.
It's a lot of Christians, but ain't nothing like Jesus,
It's "B" if you Blood
It's "Cuz" if you Crippin'
It's murder on a rival when he's caught slippin'.
But we all Black, so why are we trippin'?
It's "Us" killing us, we'll killing off our own people
That only separates us, we'll never be equal.
We living wild and foul like savage beasts
Can anybody tell me when the madness gonna cease?
Being smart is really not that hard, it's plain and simple,
There's a wealth of knowledge to be gained
In the house of the Moorish Science temple.
A prison knife, some drugs or wine...
Is that all you got to offer me?
Thanks, but I don't want it.
I got the life teachings of The Most Honorable Elijah Muhammed.
People say, "Brother, you are very intelligent, smart and full of knowledge,
"Say where did you get that wisdom?"
I got it, while I was
"IN PRISON..."

"Come Together For Unity..."

Brothers we all family
We come together for one common goal,
To make a sacrifice to cleanse our soul.
The purpose in life is to live young and grow old,
But why is our hearts so cold towards one another?
Black Men don't recognize their own brother
We act like we don't even have love for our own,
Sisters, daughters, sons, and brothers,
Won't think twice about crossing or killing their
Mother...
We quick to kill and murder another over
Simple, senseless, foolish things like colors,
Red and Blue? Brothers unaware that those colors don't
represent Me or You
We put so much energy representing a block or a rag...
Young Brothers are dying and killing each other in the streets...
To many bodies being covered in White Sheets
"Did I say white sheets?
Kinda reminds me of the Ku Klux Klan
That use to be them murdering, lynching our
Ancestors in those bloody sheets...
But wait a minute, it ain't them now,
It's "Us" killing Us more than them...
We gotta wake up Black Men
And start being righteous leaders...
Can't y'all see ain't too much change
We thinking wit all muscles and less Brain...
So many loose links, weaken the whole chain...

Russell McKinnon

We must tighten it up Black man.
We're like the hunter's getting captured By the game,
We've been kidnapped and held
Hostage by F.B.O.P
These folks don't have no love for you or me...
So, we must come together for
"UNITY"

"Demons and Devils..."

They say it takes a mighty, strong people to build a nation...
But what happen to love and creation inside of civilization,
One nation, Liberty and Justice for all,
Now take a look at America, she's about to Fall,
Donald Trump wants to build a wall...
Country lead by demon's and a devil
I'm not talking about one with a pitchfork and a shovel...
You best to know that this Devil is rich powerful sick and wicked,
They crooks by the book...
They don't give a damn about the poor like you and me
That ole mighty dollar and evil is the only thing they see...

You see Bush didn't give a damn about our people
in Hurricane Katrina and that's a fact
Don't believe me take a look at Iraq,
Young men and women lost their lives, was being under attack,
Because Bush had a grudge, he was toting on his back
It took over 10 years before the America Soldiers were bought back,
Look at the Penitentiaries all of them are fill and packed with Blacks...
Society is filled with opium, dope fiend Sisters and brothers, smoking crack...
Young black men dying and glorifying
Drugs, guns, money, murder, gangs, and violence,
Killing off each other while they remain silent.
Our Beautiful Black women glamorizing

Sex, money, and drugs
They ain't hardly got no feelings for the word of
"LOVE"
What happened to the love and unity that use to be in our community?
It used to be "Black-Power" and love for each other,
Now it's a pitiful shame that jealousy, envy, and greed
Got us pit against the other
We gotta Rise-up and wise-up and stop fooling ourselves
Because this Country is lead by "Demons and devils"...

"Nation Of Islam..."

Can anybody tell me why we live in a world of devastation, What's the illusion and confusion, to all the aggravation.
Every Country and nation want to possess Weapons of Mass Destruction
And why is every courtroom in America so full of corruption?
Where there's peace, there is war...
What are they really fighting for?
America been terrorizing on the Middle East soil
Shedding innocent blood sacrificing young men and women lives for the sake of oil.
You're witnessing wickedness at its highest level
There's no force of evil on planet earth
Worse than these American devils
Look at the death of the soldiers been slain
Was it really worth the life of Saddam Hussein?
It's crazy, it's insane, to think we are living right
We're so backwards, we don't know our days from our nights
What's the plan, what's the plight?
The low-level people at the bottom of the barrel
Get scapegoated while the masterminds walks away when Obama term was up
I knew we would pay the price
A white cop shoot and kill a black person
And beat the case...
Brother's, This poem is like rap you will never Hear on you MP3 nor see on BET
So sound off the alarm and give it up
To the Honorable Minister Louis Farrakhan
And all the fruit brothers and sisters in the "Nation of Islam"

Russell McKinnon

"Lockup But still living...

When you lockup you got to stay focus
And do some positive things,
Maintain and stay in your own lane
Don't get caught up in these penitentiary games.
To pass time I read and write especially when it's hot
I stay plotting a come up a lot
Not against another brother
I'm concentrating on staging a comeback
So, once I'm free I won't have to return.
Man, I tell you this barbaric penitentiary life it ain't no joke
I've seen weak minded prisoners under pressure
Hang themselves with a rope
I've seen men slit their wrists and slice their fucking throats
Due to the stress of this prison life they couldn't cope.
Some prisoners drink, some do dope to escape
The reality of this madness
You have a lot of lunatics in prison who ain't got a lick of sense
They will take your life for a postal stamp the equivalent of 50 Cent
I'm locked up around rapist, gang bangers, drug-dealers, parasites, and psychopathic killers
This jungle is full of traps, weapons, predators, and prey,
Menaces serving one, two, and three or more life sentences
Some forever and a day
It be all type of politicking going on here on
These state and USP-Penitentiary yards
You have to be wise not to make the wrong
Decisions not to bump heads, cars can have
A Fatal collision,

Being Locked Up ~ Prisoner's Stories *Cashville*

There's a lot of rules to the convict code,
I've seen men come in young and leave out
Old.
I know prisoners that wish they had numbers behind their sentence,
If no relief comes through the Appeals Courts, their life is finished
You got to be extra careful not to play the wrong games, all the decks are stacked
Playing the wrong games can get you attacked
A knife stuck in your back,
Or it can get your life jacked
By a person you just met or don't even know
Because in this environment that's just how it goes
Keep a shank at all times, it's a must,
Because in here you don't know Who to trust
Be wise and be your own man
Don't let another man lead you by the hand.
There's a lot of miserable people trying to tell Another man how to do his time
Blind leading the blind, they all running out of time
Being a convict you keep yourself in check
Maintain and stay in your own lane is what a wise man do
You do the time, don't let the time do you...
A spiritual man will pray to his God in peace
For it be His will, when I'll get release
I can't wait to get out of this Federal Prison
Man, this place is the belly of the beast
I can't wait to get out of this federal prison,
I'm lockup, but still living...

ABOUT THE AUTHOR

Author Russell McKinnon has spent more than 30 years of his adult life staring down hard times of prison/ incarceration toiling as a shrewd, young shark in the deep waters of life, but he knows that the race is not won by the swift and fast, but by the one who endures to the end.
Slow and steady, can win the race.

Struggle and sacrifice goes hand and hand, to be alive in a cold and unforgiving world, is to struggle and to survive, you have to strive daily in constant motion moving forward. Prison is a mental mind-set, although you are bound physically, but with the right mind-state, you can be free.

Freedom is not a place, freedom is not a thing, it's a state of being, no one can enslave you, but you.

I was in a University beyond bars...and living in the past could not create my future, so I figure out while in prison how to utilize my time wisely and constructively, seeking out my purpose for life and seizing every opportunity I could to think outside the cell that held me hostage. I spend majority of my time re-building my characteristics, restoring my life. I had to change directions with my life in a more positive and constructive manner to break the vicious cycle of being a victim to the penal system. I have a passion for writing. I learn many great lessons in life and one quote is: "You can't keep thinking the same way, doing the same thing and expect to get a different result".

We Help You Self-Publish Your Book
You're The Publisher And We're Your Legs.
We Offer Editing For An Extra Fee, and Highly Suggest It, If Waved, We Print What You Submit!

Crystell Publications is not your publisher, but we will help you self-publish your own novel.

Don't have all your money? …. No Problem!
Ask About our Payment Plans
Crystal Perkins, MHR
Essence Magazine Bestseller
We Give You Books!
PO BOX 8044 / Edmond – OK 73083
www.crystalstell.com
(405) 414-3991

Plan 1-A 190 - 250 pgs $719.00   Plan 1-B 150 -180 pgs $674.00
Plan 1-C 70 - 145pgs $625.00

2 (Publisher/Printer) Proofs, Correspondence, 3 books, Manuscript Scan and Conversion, Typeset, Masters, Custom Cover, ISBN, Promo in Mink, 2 issues of Mink Magazine, Consultation, POD uploads. 1 Week of E-blast to a reading population of over 5000 readers, book clubs, and bookstores, The Authors Guide to Understanding The POD, and writing Tips, and a review snippet along with a professional query letter will be sent to our top 4 distributors in an attempt to have your book shelved in their bookstores or distributed to potential book vendors. After the query is sent, if interested in your book, distributors will contact you or your outside rep to discuss shipment of books, and fees.

Plan 2-A 190 - 250 pgs $645.00   Plan 2-B 150 -180 pgs $600.00
Plan 2-C 70 - 145pgs $550.00

1 Printer Proof, Correspondence, 3 books, Manuscript Scan and Conversion, Typeset, Masters, Custom Cover, ISBN, Promo in Mink, 1 issue of Mink Magazine, Consultation, POD upload.

We're Changing The Game.
No more paying Vanity Presses $8 to $10 per book!

Made in the USA
Monee, IL
23 January 2022